OPEN SKY PRESS
ANNOUNCES

In July 2015 Premananda decided to go back to his given birth name, John David.

john david
(formerly Premananda)

"This change comes after 10 years of having the name Premananda, given by my friend Swami Satchitananda, master of Anandashram in Kerala. The unconditional love pointed to in 'Premananda' has become embodied in my life and continues to expand.

The name change reflects a recent inner shift and the expansion of my outer work in the Open Sky House Communities in Ukraine and Spain."

www.openskypress.com

The Great Misunderstanding

Chapter Symbols

Premananda

The Great Misunderstanding

*Discover Your True Happiness
With A Simple New Understanding*

OPEN SKY PRESS
www.openskypress.com

The Great Misunderstanding

Published by Open Sky Press Ltd.
483 Green Lanes, London N13 4BS
office@openskypress.com

Open Sky Press Distribution
Rheinstr. 54, D-51371 Hitdorf
Germany

All rights reserved. No part of this book may be used or reproduced in any part whatsoever without written permission. For further information please contact Open Sky Press.

First edition

© Open Sky Press Ltd. 2012

ISBN 978-0-9570886-7-2

Cover design by Tara
Cover portrait by Vishnu
All paintings by Premananda
Chapter symbols by Sangeetha
Photographs: Open Sky House Archive

Printed in China

OPEN SKY PRESS
www.openskypress.com

Acknowledgements

Open Sky Press has received so much support from friends and residents of Open Sky House in putting out this book, *The Great Misunderstanding*.

Over the last twelve years, audio files of my meeetings have been sent to friends living in India who ably transcribed them. In the past this was done by Aruna, Sathya and Dev Gogoi. More recently Shiva has organised a larger team adding Meenakshi and Daemian.

Devi, Mahima and Amrit sifted through the mounds of transcriptions, sorting and choosing the material to be edited. Great thanks for the love and care they lavished on this enormous task. In addition, Amrit set the scenes of my life and, with great skill, chose all the jokes.

The beautiful design of the book was done within Open Sky Press by Atma, Sangeetha and Tara. The formatting was done by Atma, under intense deadline pressure. The incredible chapter symbols and small text marks were created by Sangeetha. Tara designed the cover over days of intense colour printing to get it all just right. She also chose and laid out the amazing pages of community photographs. The website companion to this book and film was created by Durga.

Mahima nurtured this project, managing the team of translators for the German edition with infinite patience. In the hectic production phase she organised the printer, chose the paper, wrote the specifications and ensured all aspects of the printing flowed smoothly. Indira joined her in the production phase, taking over management of the translation.

Devi, a long time member of Open Sky House and now living in Australia, offered constant support in all aspects of producing this book. In particular as the editor of the English edition and final proof reader.

Premananda

Other Books by Premananda
Arunachala Shiva – Commentaries on 'Who Am I?'
Blueprints for Awakening – Indian Masters
European Masters – Blueprints for Awakening
Papaji Amazing Grace
Arunachala Talks

Films by Premananda
Arunachala Shiva – Commentaries on 'Who Am I?'
Blueprints for Awakening – Indian Masters
European Spiritual Masters – Blueprints for Awakening
Satori – Metamorphosis of an Awakening
The Great Misunderstanding

Other books by Open Sky Press
'Fire of Freedom' German Edition
'This' German Edition

Forthcoming books by Premananda
American & Australian Masters – Blueprints for Awakening
Planet Earth – Only You Can Save It
The Paradox – To Do or Not To Do

MOTHER INDIA

Thank You for Nourishing me
Opening my Heart
Showing me your Ancient Wisdom
Taking me to the Masters
Even Giving me my Name

Premananda

Contents

Chapter 1 [1]
What is the Great Misunderstanding?

The Wave and the Ocean 3
The Illusion of Separation

Living Under a Spell 9
Our False Identification

Mirrors in the Kitchen 14
Projection Creates Our Suffering

The Nervous Taxi Driver 19
Structures of the Mind

The Bird and the Seeker 25
The Search for Your True Self

Chapter 2 [31]
Supporting Self Awareness

Moving to Silence 33
Meditation and Self Awareness

Stepping Towards Grace 40
Associating With Truth

Seeking the Light 47
Finding a Guide to Awakening

Passing on the Flame 53
Being With an Awakened Teacher

Chapter 3 [63]
What is Real? Life is About Waking Up

Garden of Eden 65
Ego and Struggle

The Price of Happiness 72
The Fear of Survival

Dying into Whiteness 79
The Fear of Death

Be As You Are 86
Living Our True Nature

The World 92
Our Mistaken Ideas

Chapter 4 [99]
The Way of the Heart

Way of the Heart 101
Devotion, Trust and Surrender

Hopeless in the Desert 108
Letting Go and Being Present

The Navigation System 114
Guidance From the Heart

Way of Beauty 120
Rediscovering Our Senses

Conscious Parenting 127
Raising Children With Awareness

Chapter 5 [135]
How We Sabotage Ourselves

The Prison of the Mind 137
Fear and Attachment

Structures of the Mind 144
Identification and Judgment

The Ultimate Illusion 151
Love and Relationship

Living in La La Land 160
The Effects of Trauma

Chapter 6 [169]
Reminders to Stay Present

Rubbing Out the Doodles 171
Who Am I? The Value of Self-Enquiry

The King's Banquet 179
Self-Enquiry Opens Us to Freedom

Be Quiet 186
Leaving the Stories and Coming to Peace

The Importance of 'Thank You' 195
Life is a Mirror

Chapter 7 [205]
Awake and Free

Celebration and Natural Creativity 207
Celebrate Now

Soap in the Mercedes 213
The Mystery of Life

The Glimpse 219
Awakening From the Illusion

Tales of Awakening 227
Sharing Moments of Liberation

Living in Freedom 240
Paradise Now

Postscript
Open Sky House 253
International Satsang and Arts Community
An Experiment in Conscious Living

Premananda Biography 259

Introduction

The Great Misunderstanding is the result of fifteen years of sharing with hundreds, probably thousands of people in countries all around the world. It started in Sydney, Australia, in 1997 and then moved to India, the source of the ancient human wisdom that is being communicated in this book. Later the sharing continued through most Western European countries, particularly in Germany and also in Russia and Ukraine. This book contains the cream of the talks and personal dialogues held over all those years with a great variety of people from many different cultures.

During 2004, my second year in Europe, a community spontaneously grew from a retreat I held on a beautiful horse farm in the Black Forest in Southern Germany. After two years, the community moved to its current home in a charming old mansion in a village on the banks of the Rhine between Cologne and Dusseldorf. Located in the centre of Europe, it became *Open Sky House, International Satsang and Arts Community* where I have lived for the past six years. This book has been produced by a team from that community. I am completely touched by the amazing love and creativity they have shown in its production.

The project started when the team stayed together in a house at Arunachala, the holy mountain in South India that became known in the West through Ramana Maharshi. Piles of transcripts of my meetings were sifted through and sorted. As we sat together and shared ideas, the title emerged. We all felt it was just a simple misunderstanding about life that was at the root of so much unhappiness, and that it could easily change for want of a simple new understanding.

The Great Misunderstanding attempts to address our situation by exploring the common misunderstandings that have falsely conditioned our minds. Generations of wrong thought, passed on by loving elders, have shaped our ideas and beliefs. The early chapters set out in simple language the misunderstandings and their

The Great Misunderstanding

effects on our lives. They also suggest a way through to clarity and peace. In the last fifty years there has been a huge shift in human consciousness, making this kind of book necessary and timely.

Having begun the project in India, the team moved back to its home base in Germany. There the day-to-day support of the community enabled them to really focus on putting this book together. As the editor lives in Australia, and as I was often travelling around Europe sharing in Satsang meetings, the project has relied heavily on the wonders of modern technology.

Right now I am writing this introduction sitting close to the beach on the Black Sea in Crimea, Ukraine, were I am holding a Satsang retreat with participants from Eastern and Western Europe. I am constantly responding to emails from the production team in Germany, the editor in Australia and recently from our printer in China, all transmitted into my laptop through a satellite and small USB stick. At the same time urgent messages come through a barrage of text messages into my iPhone while I edit texts on my laptop. Meanwhile, several community members are sitting on the rocks down by the crystal clear sea translating the book for the German edition. Cormorants are diving for fish, sea gulls are circling and dolphins are playing around.

Only twenty years ago none of this high-powered technology was available, and most not ten years ago. Two years ago I began transmitting my meetings through the Internet and many of the audios from those meetings were sent to a team of transcribers – western friends living in India – and became part of the book. So over three continents and many cultures, this project has achieved an amazing result in a short time. In addition to the book, we have *The Great Misunderstanding* video selection beautifully edited onto our YouTube channel. As well, there are two companion films that accompany this book: *Satori, Metamorphosis of an Awakening* and *The Great Misunderstanding*. A trailer of each can be found on the DVD in the back of the book. Supported by our friends, we have film sub-titles in ten languages. Thank you, guys!

Introduction

A drunk man returns late one night from a heavy night. He drunkenly parks his car and heads to bed.
The conversation next morning:
Wife: 'There's trouble with the car. It has water in the carburetor.'
Husband: 'Water in the carburetor? That's ridiculous.'
Wife: 'I tell you the car has water in the carburetor.'
Husband: 'You don't even know what a carburetor is. I'll check it out. Where's the car?'
Wife: 'In the swimming pool!'

I have been an active member of the project, but it is such a team effort that I am slightly shy to have my name on the cover. Early on, the structure appeared. It is a mixture of scenes from my daily life, dialogues and texts. Together they give an insight into the life of our community and how I work in wildly different formats. Topical jokes have been sprinkled through the book to remind us that humour is a great friend. Public meetings are necessarily formal with me taking the role of the 'teacher' and the attendees taking roles as 'students'. This format has become a bit dated and within the community the sharing takes place between friends with a common interest: to raise our level of consciousness and to remain unattached to our mind structures by becoming increasingly self-aware.

As the community has matured over the last eight years so the level of our inner silence has increased. Creativity has blossomed and in addition to our Satsang band there is a busy art studio for clay modeling, drawing and painting. We have regular theatre, concerts and recitals, an annual arts festival and our own art gallery that exhibits a high level of fine art made from inner silence rather than the chattering mind. This book and the companion films come out of this creativity. The paintings beginning each chapter and on the cover are my own. The beautiful chapter symbols were created by a very talented resident. Somewhat surprisingly, we found that the paintings, the chapter symbols and the subject of each chapter aligned with the seven body energy chakras.

The Great Misunderstanding

The young teacher was teaching social studies to a class of young girls. As their weekend homework, she told the girls to do a good deed and report back on Monday.
On Monday morning, the first girl reported that she had bought food for a homeless person. A second girl was proud that she had seen someone drop a twenty-dollar note, and she had returned it to its owner. Another girl had spent a few hours reading to a blind person.
A group of four girls said they had helped an old lady cross the street.
'That's very nice,' said the teacher, 'but why did it take four of you?'
'Well,' said one of the four, 'she didn't want to cross the road.'

This book would not be possible without the ancient spiritual tradition of India, into which I dip each year. The many masters, both Indian and Western, that I have been so lucky to meet over the last years through the Blueprints for Awakening dialogues have so enriched my life. Osho, my first master, taught me meditation and self-awareness and derailed my dysfunctional lifestyle, readjusting my direction from the outer world of name and form to the inner. Papaji, and his own master Ramana Maharshi, brought me home. They taught me Self-enquiry and showed me how to live the simple life of presence, spontaneous and innocent in each moment. My heart-felt gratitude to all the masters for the wealth of wisdom they have brought to my life. I am deeply touched and transformed by them all.

The Great Misunderstanding project is an amazing resource for anyone who has become disillusioned with the narrow lifestyle offered in most societies. This is a call to arms. Wake up and take your place in the world of the innocents and be nourished by living consciously from your own being. What is offered in this book is a reminder to investigate for yourself the Truth of human life, in fact all life. Discover you have been lulled into accepting a robotic

Introduction

functioning based on the conditioning to which your mind has been subjected. Entertain the possibility of the attachment to the separate false self dissolving. Understand life has no point other than knowing yourself to be awareness and to enjoy the play of each moment unfolding.

Premananda 2012

functioning based on the conditioning to which your mind has been subjected. Entertain the possibility of the attachment to the separate false self dissolving. Understand life has no point other than knowing yourself to be awareness and to enjoy the play of each moment unfolding.

Premananda 2012

Chapter 1
What is the Great Misunderstanding?

*Imagine the waves on the ocean.
If you identify with a wave
and you look out at all the other waves,
naturally you feel separate
from the other waves.
If you really understand it,
all those waves are always
part of the ocean.
They are never separate
from the ocean and we are never
separate from consciousness.*

Chapter 1
What is the Great Misunderstanding?

As human beings we have come to perceive ourselves as separate from the world around us. We are conditioned to believe in duality. This great misunderstanding is the source of all our suffering. If we believe we are separate then we believe that all our experiences and emotions are caused by the world and by other people. Deep inside of us we know what is true and what is not true – we only forgot it. In Truth there is just one, and in this one there is and never was any suffering.

The Wave and the Ocean 3
The Illusion of Separation

Living Under a Spell 9
Our False Identification

Mirrors in the Kitchen 14
Projection Creates Our Suffering

The Nervous Taxi Driver 19
Structures of the Mind

The Bird and the Seeker 25
The Search for Your True Self

The Wave and the Ocean
The Illusion of Separation

On the ferry from Calais to Dover, travelling to a meeting in London, I had a seat by the window with a clear view over the surrounding English Channel. Looking around I could see the endless waves surging up from the vastness below, topped with spray. Some were large and full of seaweed, engulfing other waves, while some barely emerged at all, falling at the feet of another. Even the large ones though, as suddenly as they came they merged with another or smacked the side of the ferry and sank back into the ocean. An eternity of brief individual expressions.

If you look from the point of view of a wave you could say, 'I am a wave and I can see all you other waves over there.' All my conditioning has led me to believe that I am a wave, separate from all the other waves, but looking from another perspective I see all the waves are always part of the ocean. Everything is ocean. There is no real separation. The waves are never separate from the ocean and we are never separate from consciousness.

I imagine that when a baby is in the womb it experiences no sense of separation or individuality, but complete oneness with existence through the medium of the mother. When it is born and nurtured close to the mother's body, it is still one with her. Over time, the baby's parents and carers point out and reinforce names and concepts for the baby itself as well as all the other people, objects and experiences in the baby's life. Very gradually the experience of existence changes from absolute oneness to one of separation.

This is the beginning of the game of 'me' and 'you'. As human beings we have been conditioned to see ourselves as separate, when in Truth we are one with everything, just as a wave is with

What is the Great Misunderstanding?

the ocean. As we grow up the conditioning gradually gets stronger and stronger, supported by the world we grow into and know, until without even noticing we've become separate individuals, talking about 'my' boyfriend 'my' red sports car, even 'my' life. We are completely separate. We see the world out there and here is me, completely separate.

At the meeting in London I was still so affected by the crossing and the images of the waves that the subject was fresh in my mind when a young man came to the front to talk to me.

• —— •

I often feel pressure when dealing with life. When I experience myself more open, I have a yes for what is happening. More often than not I feel uneasy and disconnected.

That's because you identify with a separate 'me'. Everything you say comes back to this 'me'. When it is closed you feel separation and when it is open you feel connectedness. What happens if you take away the 'me'?

A helplessness arises.

The helplessness is also 'me' being helpless. When you really take away the 'me', what is left?

I see that I want to hold onto it all the time. It seems like that. I want to trust, but I don't dare to.

If you take away the 'me' there is just presence. There is a mind-body entity, empty, and when something happens there is a response. This response doesn't come from 'me', but from somewhere deeper.

I haven't experienced this. If I have to decide something I feel a responsibility to stay with this 'me'. So when I meet a situation I cannot

The Wave and the Ocean

be spontaneous. It takes a lot of time to look at how I feel ... perhaps angry or friendly or cautious...and eventually some trust begins to come.

I would say you are a victim of 'me'. You see everything from the position of 'me'. Did you ever consider who this 'me' is and if you can find it?

I think it is something like a stranger.

The 'me' we generally consider ourselves to be has been created gradually over many years through conditioning, imitation and identification. We could call it the false self. We experience the world from this illusory 'me', and we absolutely believe in it and identify with it. Sometimes it is trusting and sometimes not trusting. The result is what you are describing – separation.

Then the question arises, 'If I am not who I think I am, this 'me' who I identify with, then who am I?' When we do this investigation we discover that the false self, or the small 'I', exists only as memories from the past or projections into the future.

It is all those memories, ambitions, desires, hopes and fears. As we go through our day we relate to everything we meet from this 'I'. We are busy with our concepts, ideas and beliefs and we are trying to control or manipulate our lives to be what 'I' want.

Through examining the false self all our wrong ideas and beliefs fall away to reveal what we always were, what I call the Self or the eternal Self. We become present with life unfolding. The waves subside and we see the great blue ocean that was always there. That's who we are. It was just a great misunderstanding, a wrong identification.

I lived in Tokyo for three years in my late twenties and I often had a terrible feeling of separation. This time in Japan turned out to be very important for me because it made me look at myself, which

What is the Great Misunderstanding?

I'd never done before. I started to look at myself in the mirror of the Japanese. I began to see the British conditioning that I had unquestioningly identified with my whole life.

This identification, where we identify as a wave rather than the ocean, is what we call the ego. We're identifying with something that we ourselves have constructed through the normal processes of growing up and the influences of family, friends, society, religion and culture. This is completely natural, and of course if everyone around us is busy constructing their ego then we would put all our effort into it also. Within society there is so much support for the ego that we don't see the construction or that it is false.

> *A man, late for an important meeting, was searching desperately for a parking spot in a crowded car park. Looking up to the sky he entreated, 'Lord, if you find me a parking spot I promise to start going to church again.' The words were barely out of his mouth when a spot opened up right in front of his car. The man looked back up, 'Never mind. I found one.'*

The stronger we can create our ego the more successful we can be in what we want to achieve. We can become the boss, the prime minister, or the richest person. There is also the other sort of ego, which makes itself small and wants to be a victim, a loser. Whichever way, everybody is in competition. We feel we have to defend this construction, this fortress that we have built.

This construction inside our mind is reflected in the world. You can see it everywhere. When we build ourselves a house, first we build a big fence – this defines the edges of the ego – and then a big gate at the front. Maybe we install a video security camera or security guards to protect our fortress.

Sometimes we open up the gate to our fortress and invite our friends in. This is a group of people who have the same kinds of ideas as we have. They do the same kinds of things and they totally support our identity. They wear the right clothes, they go to the same places and they absolutely reinforce our idea of ourselves. Then there's another group of people – enemies. Of course, the gate doesn't open for them. Those are the people whose ideas are really different from our ideas, so they don't get invited into our fortress.

Looking at your ego can be extremely uncomfortable because everyone loves their ego construction. After all, you believe this is you. This is your life's work. Your greatest construction, 'my' life, 'me', is exactly what is in the way; it prevents you from living in freedom, from living in your true nature.

You don't have to do anything to be who you are. This is true wherever you are in life, on whatever path you are travelling. On the spiritual path, you are inexplicably drawn to something far more profound than what you know yourself to be. But even when you become a spiritual seeker, what you are seeking is who you have always been.

The only thing that prevents you from seeing this is your identification with the false self. Everything that you believe and all your ideas and judgments are simply in the way. You are conditioned with certain ideas. You call them 'my' ideas, but if you really start to examine them you quickly discover that most of them are really other people's ideas, which you are simply repeating. When something happens in your life you react from those ideas and beliefs. That's more or less how we all live. If you are very honest you can see that you are a kind of conditioned robot. That's not so comfortable, of course.

If you have never heard this before it could be really shocking because it means that everything you've identified with is not true – it's an illusion. This illusion has been created inside your own mind. It is like a film playing twenty-four hours a day the whole year, for your whole lifetime, but you are the only one watching it. Everybody else is busy watching their own film, and so we all feel separate. To maintain this duality takes a lot of effort, but everybody is doing it.

The reality is you were never separate. You've always been part of the whole. It may not appear like that because when you look around you see many bodies and it's easy to feel that you are separate,

What is the Great Misunderstanding?

but if you really understand then it's not like that. You would never consider the waves to be separate from the ocean, and, in the same way, you are never separate from consciousness. You are absolutely one with it.

Living Under a Spell
Our False Identification

Going to see the new Harry Potter film, I invited Edward, one of the teenagers from the community, and a friend of mine, Luc. As the lights went down and the film began, Edward immediately forgot his box of popcorn and his fizzy drink. Glancing sideways I could see how quickly absorbed he was. He forgot the chair beneath him and he forgot the empty screen that had been there a minute before. He was totally absorbed in the beautiful, dancing images and magical story that beamed out of the projector onto the screen and flooded into his imagination. He jumped in fear when a monster appeared, he cried at the tragedies, and he laughed with the good times. He was completely and utterly *in* the movie.

After the film we headed back home in the car. Edward was dozing in the back with his headphones on, and Luc was sitting in the front with me. We started chatting about the film, and soon got on to a topic closer to his heart than wizards and spells.

I hope you are not bored if I come back to the 'I'. I can always feel my 'I', my personality, like something solid inside me, and I can feel how it reacts and how I just go along with it and get completely caught up. I never know how to come out of it!

Being identified with the 'I' is a bit like playing a part in the movie we just saw. Let's say you're the villain! You put on a costume and you play your particular character according to the script. Gradually, this character becomes your day-to-day reality. You take on this role

9

What is the Great Misunderstanding?

and you call it 'my life'. You do it quite unconsciously, without ever really seeing what's happening.

When you live without being identified with the 'I', you're not playing any role. It's like an absence of a character and life unfolds in presence from moment to moment.

Sometimes there is an 'I' and sometimes there is no 'I'. If I start to think about how I am attached to 'I', then I feel pain.

We believe we are the doer of our lives: 'I am in control and I decide what I will do and when.' If you lift your arm, you probably think 'I am raising my arm.' If I believe that 'I' am raising my arm then I am identified with this 'I' who is doing something. This will lead to suffering. Not immediately maybe, but as you said, it brings pain when there are thoughts about it.

If you believe that 'I' am raising my arm then you are identified with this 'I' who is doing it.

But in real life I have to do things.

I probably answered twenty emails today. I had two or three meetings. I got the car fixed before picking up Edward, and so on. So a lot has happened today, but 'I' didn't do it.

What happens when you go to the cinema? Up until the movie starts you are aware of your seat, your popcorn, your drink and the empty screen. The lights go down and suddenly the screen is covered in colours and activity. At that point you're aware that this is coming from the film projector. You notice there isn't much popcorn left and maybe you even spill your drink and feel a sticky patch on your sock. You understand that the film you are about to see is only a fantasy.

As the film progresses, quite quickly you become completely absorbed. You might identify with one of the characters or you might

Living Under a Spell

just get lost in the action of the film, but quite soon you have lost the awareness of yourself sitting in a seat watching a movie. When the credits roll and the lights go up maybe you are a bit shaken, because at that point you have already become a spy, an adventurer or a superhero, and from your own perception there was no separation between you and the character on screen. Then suddenly the film is over and you are back sitting in your chair clasping an empty popcorn box and feeling something sticky on your sock.

Everyone else is leaving the cinema so maybe you blink a few times, stand up, and then, in a rather vulnerable way, make your way outside. When you get into the street, which is rather familiar, you feel normal again: 'Oh! It was only a movie!' Everyone knows the movie in the cinema was just light passing through plastic film, but what you see and experience when you emerge from the cinema you take as real. I am suggesting that what you call 'my life' is actually only a film playing in your head and is about as real as the latest Harry Potter movie.

We came onto this planet as a very small bundle, a little baby, a bit like a blank screen, and then we were taken over by our conditioning, and so our story began. The story is different depending on which culture we were born into, which religion or political situation. It might be a tragic story or it might be a heart-warming, joyful story – but usually it's somewhere in between.

This story we find ourselves cast into happens so naturally that we don't even realise. The ego develops and gradually we perceive ourselves and the world from our particular story. This story is like a spell. It feels completely normal because we're one hundred percent identified with our particular role in it. We are the main actors, we have designed our own costumes, we are the producers and the directors, and of course we are the main audience. Actually we're the only audience because everyone else is busy creating and acting out their own stories.

If I were a wizard like Harry Potter and I cast a spell on you, you wouldn't know I'd done it. You would only know you had been under the spell when you came out of it. It's the same with the ego. It's very

What is the Great Misunderstanding?

hard to see it when you're in the ego believing yourself to be a separate somebody and believing the movie playing in front of your eyes.

Whether the movie is dramatic or not, almost everybody is under the spell, completely identified with their particular role in the movie of 'my life'. This is the essence of what we have to see to become free. We have to get around the corner of our own life and see that this incredible movie that we are starring in is just a fantasy. It doesn't make a lot of difference what kind of movie it is. If you want to become free and live your true nature, then you have to see the fantasy of your movie.

When we are under the spell of the movie we act out our part in a completely unconscious way. Our behaviour always fits in with the particular story that we are in. We all know this.

When we come to the point of beginning to see our story it can be quite shocking because we notice things that perhaps we don't particularly like. We even wonder, 'Why am I doing that?' Yet we keep doing the same thing because we are absolutely identified with the role that we've assumed in our movie. Understanding this intellectually is a good beginning, because if you keep believing in the reality of your role it's very hard to come through to what is real.

Actually it's very, very simple, but it seems to be complicated because our movie is complicated. It's a strange paradox that on one hand we're searching for the Truth, love, peace and emptiness that is our true nature, and at the same time we're equally strongly running away from it. We'd rather believe our movie. We're moving towards knowing who we are and at the same time we're creating a kind of smokescreen, preventing us from really meeting it.

When you recognise your true nature free from its acquired role, without doing anything at all, everything changes. Everything is different, yet the same. Your movie has a kind of momentum and so it goes on, but it doesn't have the same bite anymore. It's like shadows that can't grab you. Even if your movie is telling you that you're small and hopeless, just a victim of life, you know it is just a story and is not true. We have many such stories.

My suggestion is that you need some help to get out of the

Living Under a Spell

spell – you need another magician to come along (called a spiritual teacher) who can see your movie and can guide you to see it yourself.

> *An aspiring monk wanted to find a guru. He went to a monastery and the guru told him: 'You can stay here but we have one important rule – all students observe the vow of silence. You will be allowed to speak to me once every twelve years.'*
> *After practising silence and meditation for twelve long years, finally the student could say his one thing, and he said: 'The bed is too hard.' After another twelve years of hard silent meditation, he had the opportunity to speak again. He said: 'The food is not good.' Twelve more years of hard work passed. His words after thirty-six years of practice: 'I quit.'*
> *His guru quickly answered: 'Good, all you have been doing is complaining.'*

Let all the stories fall away. Don't keep going back there. The invitation is simply to *be here now* – be present, here, in this moment. If you practise this, these old movies that seem so real in their intensity will start to feel less and less fixed, less and less real.

The whole spell is broken as soon as you see it clearly, and then it's over. The spell will be broken when you awaken from your identification with a fantasy. When you identify with the empty screen it doesn't matter what is projected onto it because you know that you are the screen and not the movie.

It's very common when people become Self-realised that they laugh a lot. You can laugh for two or three days at the joke of it all: believing yourself to be somebody for years and years and then suddenly – bang! – you see it was absolutely not true. This is an enormous joke.

Mirrors in the Kitchen
Projection Creates Our Suffering

I wake up at around eight to a clear morning and the spontaneous sounds of the birds. The wide sweep of the mighty river flows endlessly past the window and there is a tremendous sense of space and emptiness. I watch the constant stream of large ships passing on the Rhine, contrasting with the hobby yachts moored in the small harbour outside my window.

Sipping a cup of my favourite Earl Grey tea and sitting in the warm sun streaming through the window, I find myself reflecting on a woman who has been staying in the community for the last ten days. She told me yesterday that she was upset about the way the woman in charge of the kitchen was treating her. She went so far as to say she was bossy, even evil! While she was just trying to be friendly and helpful the other was being very nasty and trying to invade her personal space. This behaviour is a great example of projection.

Projection means to imagine that another is responsible for something that goes on inside you. If you want to put an end to suffering in your life you have to take responsibility for it. It has nothing to do with anybody out there. Realising that is a very big step because we spend most of our time projecting onto others and blaming them for our misery.

Putting an end to our habit of projection involves looking honestly at our behaviour and patterns, without judgment and opinion. We don't have to change them; we just have to see them. As soon as they are seen they are not just automatic anymore. We stop being robotic, no longer just victims of our conditioning, and we become present with life as it actually is, not as we imagine it to be.

A little old lady goes to the doctor and says, 'Doctor, I have this problem with passing gas, but it really doesn't bother me too much. It never smells and it's always silent. As a matter of fact I've passed gas at least twenty times since I've been here in your office. You didn't know I was passing gas because it doesn't smell and it's silent.'
The doctor says, 'I see. Take these pills and come back to see me next week.'
The next week the lady comes back. 'Doctor,' she says, 'I don't know what you gave me, but now my passing gas … although still silent, it stinks terribly.'
'Good,' the doctor said. 'Now that we've cleared up your sinuses, we'll start to work on your hearing.'

The reason why we don't want to see our tendency to project is that it nearly always involves some pain. We've been conditioned to always want nice feelings. So of course we are not inviting anything that could be painful, in fact we're avoiding it by projecting it onto somebody else. I invited the woman who had been so upset for a walk along the river and we talked about the way projection operates in her life.

From what you've told me, it seems you've experienced many crooks in your work and everyday life. They weren't nice people, and they did 'horrible' things to you. So you've come here, a second time now, but it's clear you're still thinking, 'Well, let's see. Let's give it another go. But probably they're also crooks and criminals and they'll also exploit me or do horrible things!'

Now you've even managed to make Darya into a criminal! It's almost impossible to make Darya into a criminal, you see, because she's spent most of her life taking old ladies across the road! She's the last person you could ever imagine as a crook!

What is the Great Misunderstanding?

She's not so nice!

Right. She's not so nice. Although she's so nice that we've often told her to start being a bit more nasty.

Well, she's started!

But in your eyes she was already a horrible, nasty person! What do you think that is? Is that true? Or is that to do with you? It must be to do with you, because you've been so brutalised by life that you are ready to believe that even Darya could be horrible. You have the same idea about the world. You make it threatening, full of thieves and people who want to cheat you.

You move from place to place looking for answers and searching for inner peace, but you are constantly suspicious. There is not much trust. If you're going to blame the world, if you're going to blame somebody else, you have no chance to get out of your suffering.

The first step is that you take responsibility for that inside you that blames the world and other people. You probably want to run away at the moment, but if you really don't want to have this suffering in your life you'll need to find a place where you can feel relaxed, safe and supported, and where things will happen in an authentic way. But it's not going to always be nice! It can't always be nice!

Yes. Darya really gets to something inside me. She's so tense and reactive and she doesn't even know it.

There are all kinds of mirrors offered here in this community through all the different people. If you accept these mirrors, and accept your reflection, you will start to see yourself and something can change in you. But it's not a five-minute job, so you need some trust and willingness to be available for this process.

Yes, I saw something but now it's disappeared.

Mirrors in the Kitchen

It's just funny that you ended up working with Darya in the kitchen, and that you are clearly strong mirrors for each other. You see, it's so lovely how existence works!

•⎯⎯⎯•

I then left her to walk on her own with the birds and the wide fields bordering the river. Later she was back in the kitchen laughing and chopping carrots, with her mirror, Darya, doing the very same standing opposite her.

Later that day, sitting alone in the courtyard and watching the peacocks wander around the grounds, I went over the reasons why this woman couldn't be happy and at peace.

Everyone always judges and is absolutely not content with where they are, what they are doing or who they are with. They always wish to be some other place, because somewhere else is bound to be better than it is here. If you project this discontent and unhappiness onto somebody else, you avoid taking the responsibility for that being you. You can say, 'She is doing something to me,' but that's a little bit of a cop-out because you have a choice. When something comes up you can say, 'It's her fault I feel like this,' or you can say, 'Actually, there is something in me that I can look at.'

The horrible truth is it is never the other. It is always your projection. Nobody ever does anything to you. You don't want to believe that because you like to blame all your suffering on somebody else.

It is so easy to believe that somebody has given us our pain. What if you would see that the pain is helping you and is not against you? For example, if you cut your finger then the body gives you pain and you can take care of the wound. Equally, if you come into a drama, the emotional pain is showing you that you have a wound that needs attention.

This emotional wound comes out of an attachment you have to some situation from your childhood that remains inside you. It is not caused by someone else. They can be a trigger for it, but what's been triggered is already something inside you. Often just coming into a situation immediately brings up this pain.

While you are caught up in the illusion of the 'I', your conditioned, unconscious habits will keep putting you into pain. The only way out of the pain is through self-awareness. Gradually you will find that you don't have to go into it. If you have achieved some real inner silence then it is much easier to watch the pain with some distance.

In the context of spiritual freedom, you have to come to a point where you accept the pain. Probably the fear of the pain is much worse than the actual pain. You're afraid that someone could do something to you because you believe yourself separate from that person who is going to do it. It always comes back to this false identification.

Life is beyond pain and happiness. When you stop all your effort of resisting what is, then suddenly life is really incredible! It's not that everything turns to gold, or all the trees start to blossom out of season and drop petals on your head. It's not like everyone suddenly loves you. It's just that everything is absolutely accepted, and every ordinary thing becomes very beautiful.

The Nervous Taxi Driver
Structures of the Mind

One year ago a young woman moved into the community and has since become one of the most competent people in the house, in charge of many different projects and tasks. Felicia does her work beautifully and with interest. However, she has a tremendously strong pattern inside that tells her she is not good enough. This results in a solid 'victim' mentality, and so she is often very much caught up in emotional dramas. Luckily she is aware enough of these patterns that recently she came and talked to me about what was happening. We sat in the art gallery, a lovely part of our community house, and had tea together.

Today, after lunch, there was a little moment of calm as I was sitting quietly alone, but then someone came and asked for something and immediately the whole thing started again. It's so quick, and it creates so much stress! There's so much fear and anger against everything that I just get lost. I have a little inner voice that sometimes guides me back to presence and some clarity, but then the next thing happens and I completely forget and the other messages, like 'not good enough', come up immediately!

Why do you hold on to all the rest of it? Why don't you just stay with this inner voice?

I just forget.

What is the Great Misunderstanding?

Are you giving this voice a proper priority? Or are you always choosing the old story?

When I'm caught up in my working day I just forget that there is an inner voice. I can't remember anymore! It's like I'm a completely different person who can't remember.

Put a reminder on your computer: 'Here I am!' It would make a big difference to your life if you were to remember this part of you, because this is you. This is your essence. And all this other stuff that goes on – all this drama and blah blah – you really don't need this in your life anymore. It can all be dropped. Completely dropped.

After this talk I saw her change to some extent, but she would very quickly get caught up and forget the advice I had given and what we had talked about. I didn't talk to her again in this personal way until some months later, during a Satsang broadcast from our annual Indian retreat.

We were broadcasting the meeting using little internet sticks for reception and bottles of insect spray against the mosquitoes. Felicia came through via Skype into the meeting and shared briefly that for the last few days she had been completely engulfed in her many dramas, making her life difficult and stressful.

In an effort to help her be more aware of it all, I tried to lay out exactly what I could see was going on inside her. Obviously the previous meeting had not shown her clearly enough.

Let's take a look at what's happening. You are taking everything around you as real and yourself as separate from objects and people. You allow yourself to be swamped by all kind of emotions. All this emotional reaction is mind. A thought comes, quickly followed by an emotion.

The Nervous Taxi Driver

This is the way that you stay separate. It's a deep strategy that has been there for most of your life. Together with this is the feeling that 'somebody is doing something to me'. Actually, nobody is doing anything to you. You are doing it to yourself, constantly, and if you look honestly you will see that.

You are always checking on the outside. It makes you very involved with others: 'Where are they? How are they doing? How am I doing in comparison?' One of your mind structures is 'I'm not good enough'. This doesn't mean you are not good enough – it's just your mind telling you that.

Bringing more meditation and silence into your daily life would be very helpful for you. We are so programmed to relate and to tell our story: how we feel, how we would like it to be, and couldn't we just change it all, and blah, blah, blah. We have so many important things that we have to put out into the world. We want everybody to know our strong feelings about everything.

The invitation is to stay with the silent part, to look and find out what doesn't change. To really get in touch with that you will find it helps to be quiet, not to be talking or activating the stories and structures. When you are more empty and quiet you'll be able to see for yourself what is going on. This is called self-awareness, and it's important for you now to develop this quality.

Basically, you don't want to allow what is there. You always find a diversion so you don't really have to look at what is happening. You do something to avoid seeing it, to cover it up and to pretend it's not there. But the best thing you can do is to absolutely accept it. It's not wrong. It's just what's happening.

When you always do something to hide what the feeling is, everything gets very complicated. When you completely accept whatever is happening, one hundred percent, this will really start to change something in your life. You don't have to do anything. Just see it. Just watch. You don't have to change the patterns or say they aren't good. You don't have to judge them. Just accept them as they are.

For you it's more than 'not good enough'. Your structure easily puts you into a victim mentality and then you think somebody else

What is the Great Misunderstanding?

is creating that in your life. Self-awareness will help you to see that this is completely not true. The key to self-awareness is to sit in silence several times throughout the day. The outer quiet will give you more inner quiet.

In a rational sense, everybody knows that you do a lot of tasks very beautifully in the community. You would probably find that everyone thinks you're good enough. This is one kind of reality, but this doesn't help you because you have your own structure that's feeding you the wrong information all the time – that you're not good enough. As the day progresses it's as if you're looking for things that will prove you are not good enough. You become a victim. Everything is conspiring against you. When you really see this mechanism it will dissolve by itself.

Nothing has to change on the outside for you to feel good inside. All your problems and dramas are created by the structures within your own mind. I came across the perfect joke for you and your emotions!

> *A passenger in a taxi leaned over to ask the driver a question and tapped him on the shoulder. The driver screamed, lost control of the cab, nearly hit a bus, drove up over the curb and stopped just inches from a large plate glass window. For a few moments everything was silent in the cab, and then the still shaking driver said, 'I'm sorry but you scared the daylights out of me.'*
> *The frightened passenger apologised to the driver and said she didn't realise a mere tap on the shoulder could frighten him so much. The driver replied, 'No, no, I'm sorry, it's entirely my fault. Today is my first day driving a taxi…I've been driving a hearse for the last twenty-five years.'*

She could laugh at herself then, and said she could see how, like the taxi driver, she no longer needed these strong emotional reactions because they are from the past and don't serve her anymore.

Looking back on my own story I saw how I had also had this pattern of 'not good enough' running very strongly for much of my life. I noticed one day that it had disappeared, not to be replaced by any idea that now I am good enough, but merely being in each moment as it unfolds – being as I am and not caring if it's good enough or not. Since then it has been very beautiful. Nearly everybody has, or had, this pattern. It is just incredible how common it is. Just look at Napoleon. He had to conquer most of Europe to prove that he was 'good enough'.

It seems to me that when we were children we were never really good enough for our parents. Whatever we did, it seemed like it wasn't the right thing. The child was always confused, never really knowing what was okay. This uncertainty was taken into adulthood. But it's not true. It wasn't then, and it isn't now. We are exactly as we're meant to be!

The tragedy of humanity is that we don't understand how life works. We believe in being a separate somebody and then we believe that the somebody is not okay the way it is. The reality is that in every moment we are exactly as we are meant to be. We can't be different!

You can go to the other extreme and say, 'I *am* okay!' You can do affirmations for thirty minutes every morning convincing yourself that you are okay. But it doesn't really help. Whether you think you are okay or whether you think you are not okay, you're tied into the structure of a somebody. You believe yourself to be something that simply doesn't exist. While you hold onto that belief, while you are attached to that belief, you will certainly suffer through all kinds of situations.

When that whole structure dissolves you simply are who you are, from moment to moment. There's no longer anything inside that is saying I am okay or I am not okay. If something happens during the day, you will respond to that situation in that moment in a way that will be unique to you. Everyone will respond to the situation in a different way.

What is the Great Misunderstanding?

Two monks were washing their bowls in the river when they noticed a scorpion that was drowning. One monk immediately scooped it up and set it upon the bank. In the process he was stung. He went back to washing his bowl and again the scorpion fell in. The monk saved the scorpion and was again stung. The other monk asked him, 'Brother, why do you continue to save the scorpion when you know its nature is to sting?'
'Because,' the monk replied, 'it is my nature to save it.'

The Bird and the Seeker
The Search for Your True Self

In my office I have two darkened windows that protect against the glare of the summer sun. Every morning a small bird flies to the window ledge, curious to see another bird in his territory. Fascinated by his own reflection, he hops against the glass, pecking and tweeting at the matching image. Being so close, he never touches that which he believes is there, only hitting himself where his reflection meets the mirror of the glass. Through all his efforts, he is simply confronted by a confusion of wings and bird cries, all coming from him. This continues for a few minutes then he flies away, probably a little more exasperated each time.

One day I decided to end this amusing little illusion and slid the window open while he was on the ledge. He paused, then jumped up and perched on my lamp, inside my room. He looked around, suddenly through that imperceptible barrier that had held his mirror image. He stopped for a few seconds, just there, not chasing any phantoms. Just him, breathing quietly, after all the confusion of the reflections. Then the moment passed with a chirp and a flutter as he hopped back out into the world.

The bird's misunderstanding was that it was not some other creature he was seeing. Our great misunderstanding is that we think we are the false self, the image we have created of ourselves.

The Self is a given. We come into this life empty. It is our nature. I use the word empty not in the sense of there not being anything but rather everything coming out from the Self. A kind of spontaneous joy, coming from an innocent disposition to the world. Happiness means just to be who you are. What could be more simple? What do you have to do to be who you are? You have to do something to

What is the Great Misunderstanding?

not be who you are.

Being who you are is awakening, enlightenment. So much is said about this, as if it should be something very special. The actual experience can be dramatic, but where you go to is very ordinary.

One more teaching, one more teacher, one more book or looking around one more corner won't help you find it. It will just make sure that it won't be revealed because you are looking on the outside rather than inside, and however diligently you look there, you won't find it. You hope that going on a spiritual journey will bring you something you don't have now.

We are Truth; we are what we are looking for. It's right here, so close. It's a bit like a dog chasing its own tail. The dog never realises that the tail is part of itself, and the more it runs the more the tail also runs!

This is an incredible misunderstanding. People think the tail is somehow separate and if they just get the right teaching, they will find out where the tail is and then they can stick it back on the dog. What you're looking for is *you* and it's always there. You *are* what you are searching for, so naturally the more you search for it in the outside world the further you move away from it. This totally wrong direction keeps some people in the role of spiritual seeker for thirty or forty years.

People go from teacher to teacher looking for the one with the most wisdom or the strongest presence, and they're surprised that nothing really happens for them. Yes, perhaps they experience joy, but it soon dissipates when they return to their familiar surroundings.

One such man recently visited our community. He has been completely caught in the bonds of searching for thirty years, and has found only confusion upon confusion. He came especially for evening Satsang and was the first to sit with me.

When I listen there is a lot going on in my head. I can see the identification with the 'I', which wants to search so much. I have been searching for the last thirty years. It feels as if there is not much holding me back, just …

And what would happen if you could just decide to stop now? As far as I know, you've visited every spiritual teacher in the world. You became very friendly with two or three of them, you've read nearly all the books and you've done all the practices. You even teach other people how to do them! What could be left? This must be the moment to simply stop. What's left when you stop?

I don't know who it is that can stop.

But right now, at three minutes past nine, what's going on over there *now* in this moment? It doesn't actually matter what happened in the last thirty years; that's all past and finished. It won't help you at all right now. So *right now* what's happening?

There's happiness, and sadness about all this stupid effort!

So accept it and then you can start laughing.

I was hoping so much for …

Yes, you were hoping there would be a big fireworks display and Jesus and Buddha would be standing there saying, 'Welcome! You finally got to the end of the race! Here's your Spiritual Gold Medal!'

I have the feeling that I can't believe it anymore, after so long.

You dont need to believe in anything! There's nothing to believe. You just have to see that all this striving and all these techniques and all those teachers didn't really help much. So right now what's left?

I don't know. Some clinging, just there in the mind, which doesn't want to let go. It wants to have a meaning. It can't have all been for nothing!

What is the Great Misunderstanding?

Well, the reality is that you had to do all those things in order to let them all go in this moment. Otherwise, in this moment there would be one more book or one more technique.

Yes, the clearing gets less, but deeper. There is still this idea of a personal history.

Yes, it doesn't help in this moment. Twenty years ago, on Friday afternoon, you had a cup of tea with a great master, so what? And twenty years ago on Saturday afternoon you read a wonderful spiritual book, so what? Now, *in this moment*, what's happening right now?

There's a vastness and a little bit of clinging. There's some fear about what might happen tomorrow – maybe tomorrow I will be disappointed.

Yes, but tomorrow also doesn't exist. There is only now.

• ——— •

Here we are, and there's nothing to do, there's no teaching, and so you're just left with what is, in this moment. It's impossibly simple, and if you postpone to another moment then you didn't understand. You think that you have to transform 'me', make yourself into a slightly better flavour of 'me'. As soon as you stop, then the surrender to 'what is' can just happen by itself. Real surrender means that you give yourself to existence. What does that mean? It means you simply accept what is.

Existence is not separate from what is. You are also not separate from what is. And 'what is' includes everything: emotions, feelings, everything. If you are bored, be bored. If you are happy, be happy. If you are pissed off, enjoy it. We always have the idea that we have to change pissed off into something nice. Nothing has to change. Anyway, how can you change it? You have simply to accept it as it is, but you always take the position of wanting to change it.

The Bird and the Seeker

Deep within a forest a little turtle began to climb a tree. After hours of effort he reached the top, jumped into the air waving his front legs and crashed to the ground. After recovering, he slowly climbed the tree again, jumped, and fell to the ground. He tried again and again while a couple of birds sitting on a near-by branch watched his sad efforts. Finally, the female bird turned to her mate. 'Dear,' she chirped, 'I think it's time to tell him he's adopted.'

When it rains we would like the sun to shine, and when we are sad we have the feeling we should be happy. Totally surrender. Just accept it as it is. There is a lot to do if you are trying to change it. There is nothing to do if you just accept it. We are very attached to trying to change the illusion into the perfect illusion, but a perfect illusion is still an illusion. The truth is that nothing is happening and there is nobody to do anything. Our minds find that a bit difficult because we've learned that we have to work really hard for anything of value.

Don't just accept what I tell you. Enquire for yourself by being quiet. Just by being quiet you will discover who you are. When we become quiet the thoughts become less. Gaps appear between the thoughts. In these gaps there is nothing. Then we get a little more quiet and as the gaps become larger and larger our strong identification with the thoughts begins to break down. We're not meditating, we're not repeating a mantra and we're not practising any technique; we're just being quiet.

So, wow! It may not last so long in the beginning, because naturally the thoughts have a very strong momentum. Some of us make a whole career of our dramas – our whole identity depends on them – but as you become quieter the stillness is just there, and that's you. You're not the drama, you're not the story, but in fact you're the source of the story, and this source is emptiness. Peace. Stillness. The Eternal Self. The Self. Even God. Existence Itself. Real Happiness.

Moving to Silence

When I was busy with spiritual practices there was a period when I did five hours a day of Tai Chi. A lot changed in my body and I also became more open, more fluid and more centred. It helped me to see myself in a different way and to loosen up old blocks in my system. Exercises such as Tai Chi or Yoga can be a strong support on your path, both for the body and the mind.

In the classic Indian tradition there are three types of mind. A very active and passionate mind has very little space, and a quiet, sleepy and sluggish mind has almost too much space, never quite getting to the point. The third type is a pure mind in which there are not so many thoughts any more and one no longer gets caught up in dramas but leads a very easy, quiet, peaceful life. When a big drama happens there is a space inside the mind to deal with it. Once you achieve a pure mind, harmony and peace will manifest in your life.

If you have a very strong mind then you are absolutely identified with being a separate 'somebody'. However, as you develop awareness about yourself, with the help of meditation and perhaps some physical practices, the mind becomes more quiet, still, and peaceful. In this way you are more likely to have moments when you meet your true nature.

You are able to be in a space behind the mind, behind the chatter, the judgments, the beliefs and the ideas about yourself and the world. The process of coming to this space and developing a quiet mind is not necessarily a quick or easy one, but these glimpses of your true nature will make it much easier to continue with the meditation.

The introspective quality of meditation supports you in becoming a witness to everything you experience. The witness is able to look inside and register whatever is happening. This is also called self-awareness.

Recognising the witness is a very important part of waking up. Finally the witness itself will dissolve, but before it comes to that point we need to build up the ability to watch ourselves inside. For that we also need to be very honest, because it's not so easy to always accept what we observe. Our observation should be without any

Supporting Self Awareness

'good or bad' judgments, without any judgments at all.

When we become quieter we can see how our thoughts arise. Normally, we just grab the thoughts. For example, the thought, 'I'm hungry,' could lead to remembering the fridge is pretty empty. Then the next thought might be about where to go to buy food. Then, 'Oh, how do I get there? The bicycle is broken!' So from the initial thought, 'I'm hungry,' we are thinking about how to fix the bicycle. In fact, nothing real has taken place.

With self-awareness you can see how a thought is created in the mind. If it has come from the mind it is not real. It's only an illusion. It's just a thought. You might have a thought that somebody is against you, but it is just a thought; it's not real. If you can become quiet enough and self-aware enough you can see this thought coming out of nothing and you can just leave it alone.

To further encourage self-awareness I recommend you live at a pace where you can be present. Almost for sure in the beginning you have to move slowly, because if you don't slow down you will continue to operate on automatic. When we are stressed, we immediately fall into our robotic, conditioned behaviour. We need a conscious device to bring ourselves to presence.

Make a deliberate effort to move very, very slowly – more slowly than you habitually feel to move. Moving from your car to the house like this might take ten minutes rather than two minutes. You'll be very surprised at how much you notice in these ten minutes. When you slow down, suddenly you become much more aware of whatever is around you and also of what's going on inside. There is only this moment, and if you miss this moment then you're going to miss the next moment as well. In this way you could even miss your whole life!

When I first went to an ashram in India I did a lot of meditation, and I noticed something very interesting. I started to move slowly, not because of a conscious decision but just because the meditation slowed me down. I was completely surprised to discover a whole world of insects and bugs that I had never seen before. I hardly even knew they existed! Suddenly it was like 'Wow! All these insects crawling around my breakfast table!' I had been moving too fast even to meet them.

The transition from years of unconscious living into conscious living is not so easy and of course everyone is different and everyone will need slightly different supports. Basically we all need to make quite a big effort in the beginning, but after some time it will happen by itself.

Rhyan, a young Australian guy, has been living in the community for about a year now and is very competent and confident. He had never meditated before and did not seem to really get it for the first few months he was here. It was only recently that something came up for him and he was able to look more deeply into himself and could really see how fast his motorway was running. It was clear that his meditation had given him insight into his behaviour and motivations.

I've had this thought so many times, 'I'm a piece of shit.' I can't even say how often. Probably I've thought it non-stop every day since I've been here, so there has been no pause, no gap to realise 'I think it. It's just a thought.' It is constantly there, but I never realised it was so strong.

That's really important. Every thought comes and every thought goes. If you're not totally diligent, you immediately identify with the thought. You absolutely believe the thought! So, for example, you absolutely believe that you are completely worthless. You believe the thought because you're identified with it.

For a moment I could see this. 'Look! It's there again. Ah! It's just a thought.' But it was very strange because there was this other something watching this thought.

That's the witness. Seeing that you are the witness of this thought, not the thought itself, is another level of understanding. If you can

Supporting Self Awareness

witness that thought arising then you are not identified with it. There's a very important gap between witnessing the thought arising and identifying with the thought. It really changes your life to stay with the gap; don't be tempted to pick up the thoughts. As soon as you do, you're back in the old habits.

How about when an emotion comes up? Is it that I've already caught a thought?

Yes. Usually there's the thought and then the emotion comes in response to the thought. This thought that you're completely worthless is obviously not true, is it?

When I can admit that it's nothing more than a thought, no, it's not true.

That's a huge step, whether you know it or not. You're not really caught in that thought anymore. You're no longer identified with it.

Well, I am still identified with it, but now I can observe something in myself: 'Ah! Here's something funny! It's that thought again!'

Just an odd thought. We have millions of them every day.

But sometimes I still really believe I'm a piece of shit. What should I do with that?

Well, you don't have to do anything! If you do something with it, then you're lost in the shit, you see? And you don't have to replace it with a more positive thought either. It's just a thought. It's absolutely not real!

A profound self-awareness is required and meditation is a tool that gives you the space to step back and see a thought or emotion arising. Then you can go further and direct your attention to where the thought comes from, which is out of emptiness.

None of the mind structures touch or disturb the emptiness. These ideas, 'Somebody is against me' or 'I'm piece of shit' just disappear; they melt away, along with all your other ideas, dramas and judgments.

Even the witness, which you discovered through meditation, is in the mind and will disappear in the right moment. Then there is nobody to witness anything. You are simply the stillness, the emptiness, the nothing, the absolute.

You could imagine that you came to the absolute because of meditation, but actually, you're already the absolute. You cannot not be! When you realise you are the absolute, that's it! Game over!

Many people I know would be very willing to do some really tough spiritual practice. If I said, 'Okay, if you really want peace then for three months, or even three years (some might even go for thirty years) you have to get up at five-thirty in the morning, take a cold shower and sit in meditation for two hours.' They would say, 'Great! Okay. He's a really tough teacher, but I'll do it.' But if I say you don't have to do anything and that actually it's available right now, then what?

Buddha did all kinds of very tough practices for many years. Finally he sat under a tree and gave up. In the moment of giving up he suddenly saw that he was the absolute and had always been so. It's a very simple understanding, but it's almost impossible to realise. Some people need twenty years of practice just to get so tired that they give up. Like the Buddha.

Once Self-realisation has taken place there will be no identification or attachment to the thoughts any more. The thoughts, emotions, knowledge and judgments become like clouds and we have become the open sky, peaceful and empty. The clouds can pass by without disturbing us.

Stepping Towards Grace
Associating With Truth

Welcome to Satsang. In this moment when I look inside I find a profound silence. Odd thoughts struggle to make themselves appear but the silence is so intense and deep that these thoughts are far away – they have no bite. They are more like shadows of thoughts. The mind-body entity has no interest in doing. Even the smallest doing seems like a tremendous effort. There is no interest in the outside, very little is happening. There is a tremendous sense of peace, peace without any edges or form, eternal peace. The person called Premananda is far away. There is some memory of this personality, but he feels like a character from another play, another theatre – an old story.

The Self is radiant, a deep merging and melting in this moment of sitting together. We have chosen to go on an immense journey together. A journey from nowhere to nowhere – from here to here. We are brought ever back to this moment. The presence in this moment allowing what is, seeing this unfolding, accepting it as it is.

Slowly our own struggles, our own story, our desires and fears and belief of how it should be become further and further away. Everything seems to be alright; existence has its small victories – we give them up willingly, our trust increasing, our surrender increasing, a real excitement in letting existence take over.

From the past we know the tremendous effort that was needed to keep the ship leaning into the wind, keeping it moving forward. Now we start to let that effort go, step-by-step, small victory by small victory, our trust increasing, seeing that nothing awful is happening. Actually we start to feel a little happier each day, a little more peaceful and empty. There are more smiles and laughter, less seriousness, no sadness. It's just okay the way it is; we can cope with whatever it is. It's as good as it gets right now.

Simply blissful, relaxed and peaceful. An enormous peacefulness, and we become ready to surrender our old world – my story. We just want to let it go and be an adventurer into the unknown, the unknowable, into the unfolding mystery.

These words came spontaneously at the end of our recent Summer Retreat, two weeks of intensive meetings. One of the participants was a man who has been visiting our community on and off every couple of months, a sweet man who has a real sense of what is happening in the community and the energy of the people. His first visit was to an intensive weekend retreat when he knew hardly anything of the community itself, but had an interest in knowing himself.

He lives on his own, spending time with his daughter, his hobbies and working at a job that largely fulfills him. He involves himself as much as possible in retreats, weekends and evening meetings and has even supported the running of the house with donations. By involving himself from a genuine desire and passion he is giving space for something inside him to grow, encouraging something to blossom that is hardly supported in his everyday life.

One of the ways he stays regularly in touch with me is through Skype in the live Satsang TV broadcasts that happen four times a week from our community. During the Summer Retreat he had become a kind of laughing Buddha, giggling and roaring with humour and joy for almost the whole time. Something had opened in him and he came through on Skype the day he returned home after the retreat had finished.

What to say? Just thank you.

What are you thanking me for?

Supporting Self Awareness

I don't know. I'm just so grateful because I saw myself so clearly and beautifully, and felt so at home and at peace. What can I say but thank you!

Well, I think you are grateful to have met some people here who don't accept this whole false-self story: 'my life'. You have discovered that there is the possibility to live life in another way. When it happened to me, I was twenty-nine. I'd been searching for another way to live, but had no idea what that could be. Coming into an Indian ashram when I was twenty-nine and seeing what was happening there – feeling the love, the energy and excitement for life in the spontaneous and free behaviour of the people – was a mind-opener for me. A whole bunch of people from different countries had come together and were beginning to find a new way of communing together, living together, functioning together. It was unbelievably exciting!

Maybe that's why I was not shocked when I came to your place, because at that moment everything started to make sense.

Right. We had a resident here some years ago whose family had taken her to a psychologist to 'sort her out'. She had 'strange ideas' and 'wasn't at all normal'. When she met me, she discovered that what she'd known inside for years was not 'strange' or 'wrong'. She found other people who understood her. This is a liberation, because suddenly the energy moves in another way inside you. Instead of the sense that you've 'got something wrong', you realise that maybe you've always had something right! To have the support of other people, and to have a teaching behind it so that it makes sense and gives stability, is very empowering. Maybe you're thankful for all this.

Yes, exactly! I just want to be available to something that I feel a yearning for inside.

Stepping Towards Grace

By giving your attention to Truth and being discriminating in how and where you spend your time, you've made yourself very available. If you give it permission, that opening can continue. It only depends on your 'yes' now. Sometimes when we open up there come doubts, 'buts' and fears. Something is unknowable or unknown, not familiar, and so we can become afraid. In the end, it depends on you. My message is to just let it open and let it take you. It's very beautiful. There's no end; you just move on and on.

Good.

And whatever happens is your happening. You don't have to believe anything. It's not about beliefs; it's about allowing yourself to move through what you call your life, open, available and spontaneous. At some point it simply unfolds! It's amazing!

Awakening to this easiness is in the hands of grace. If it is destined to happen it happens, and if not, it doesn't. Saying this, we do have our little choices on the way that can open us to existence and which can invite the workings of grace into our lives.

There is no doubt that if you associate with people who are aware, they will not support your continued identification with your opinions and beliefs, your old dramas and traumas. They won't give you so much energy if you are getting into one of your stories. So it's not surprising that several people in our community have had an energetic opening and in several cases this opening has continued.

Openings are not uncommon, but without this kind of support they can very quickly be lost. So clearly there is a value in associating with a group of people who are particularly focused on these things.

> *Four monks agreed to meditate in silence for a week and to not speak a single word. On the first day, they all maintained silence. But as darkness fell, the flame of their single candle*

> *began to flicker. 'Oh, the flame is going out,' said one monk.*
> *'Eh, we should not speak a single word,' said the second monk.*
> *'Why do you two want to speak?' said the third monk.*
> *'Ha! I am the only one who did not talk!' said the fourth monk.*

Who you associate with has a profound effect. You can put yourself into an environment with people who are unconscious and robotic and who actually have no interest in looking at themselves, or you can associate with people who are conscious and interested to become more conscious, and who are on the same journey as you. That will give you enormous support.

Another choice we can make which brings us closer to the possibility of an 'aha!' moment is to develop the habit of self-reflection, shifting our attention from 'out there' to 'inside'. This will require some courage because when we honestly take a look at what is happening, we might not be so happy about what we find.

If you want to release yourself from suffering, pain and unhappiness, you have to become self-aware. Examine whatever happens in your daily life. We are all busy with things that keep us focused on the world 'out there'. In modern society most of us have pressure to work, perhaps in a job that we don't particularly like. In that kind of circumstance it's very hard to look. Very rare.

As you get more and more into the habit of self-awareness, you gradually get a handle on the conditioning that you've been subjected to. You begin to see how the ideas and beliefs that result from this conditioning stand between you and who you really are. You have little insights, little moments of 'aha!' As these little moments increase, you can't really believe anymore that you are a somebody.

With this understanding you no longer need to be so caught up in your particular psychological structures. What's much more important is that by understanding the whole mechanism of identification there is a chance that you'll come to a moment where you see it so clearly that it just drops. It disappears. It's a moment of realising one hundred percent who you are.

Coming to Satsang is another thing you can do to bring you closer to the hands of grace. This meeting is all about the 'me' without any story, which comes when you are absolutely present and there are no thoughts for the past or future. Usually we are caught up with doing, thinking, remembering last week and maybe having some fear about next week – so we are never really here. But when we become quiet, just for a moment, we can settle down and come to this essence, our true me.

Satsang is a reminder that we can know who we are, and that who we are is always here. It's an incredible opportunity and a powerful support. There is no need to divide life into spiritual life and ordinary life, with one being more desirable than the other. That's the beautiful thing about life. When you are untroubled by the mind, washing the dishes is just as fulfilling and beautiful as deep meditation.

In Satsang we become quiet. We leave our stories and dramas behind for two or three hours, dropping our attachment to them and coming to stillness. When we go back to work, families, relationship, everyday life, just walking in the street we find there's a collective sense about life that we've been conditioned by for so many years. We pick up again all those invisible structures and we're back in the movie called *My Life*. Immediately the stillness seems to fade away. But we *are* that stillness. That is our nature. It's always there. We just lose touch with it.

Truth is absolutely beautiful because it's so incredibly simple. It's a complete turn around, because you don't need anything from the outside. You don't need anything from anybody. You've got it all there, everything, all the wisdom of the universe, all the knowledge, all the love, everything is just there.

When you come to Satsang you're choosing to be in *sat*, Truth. In the regular society the association is not with Truth. It is with 'me' and 'my' story and everybody else's story. It needs some clarity and commitment to stay with *sat*. In Satsang and in the community

Supporting Self Awareness

around a teacher we can experience tremendous support and love – support to stay with Truth rather than with 'my story'. If you associate with Truth, then you are closer to the hands of grace.

Seeking the Light
Finding a Guide to Awakening

Recently there was a man visiting my weekly meetings who was particularly interested to find out if I was the right teacher for him. He had romanticised the concept of finding a teacher, having read piles of spiritual books, and probably developed a whole tapestry of philosophies and ideas in his head in the meantime. He had put many questions to me in Satsang about what it means to be my 'disciple', what the work will involve and how to know if I am the right teacher. I gave him all the answers, but he was never quite satisfied.

Finally, it came to a point where he had come four or five times and had progressed no further than just asking a lot of questions. This prompted me to question his motivation: Was he interested in really finding out the answers to these questions, or was he just interested in asking them? He was trying to get me to answer the questions to his thinking mind. I wasn't interested in answering that part of him, but rather the part that had brought him here.

He was busy working with his mind on choosing a teacher, figuring out who would be best, and especially if he could trust that person. He said he had a desire to become Self-realised in this lifetime, but he was making sure everything was just right from the point of view of his mind before he could start.

It was clear from our meetings that he could not trust whatever had guided him on his search for Truth and had brought him to a place where that Truth could be realised. He was stuck in his mind and nothing was getting through to a deeper part of him.

In our last meeting I felt he was drifting away, so I spoke to him again about the process of finding the right teacher.

Supporting Self Awareness

If you have a connection to your Self, then a teacher on the outside could be unnecessary. However, most of us are so identified with being a somebody that we need a living somebody on the outside to guide us. The disciple goes through his own inner process, and when he sincerely comes to a moment where the priority of Truth is so strong that he can't really help himself, then the teacher appears, just like some sort of magic show. When you are ready inside, the teacher appears.

It's hard to accept that I have no choice or responsibility in choosing who that teacher is. It makes it difficult for me to surrender.

Openness is essential. Whether the heart is really open and whether there is some trust and later surrender, this all happens by itself. You can't really do any of those things.

You say that for ten years you were reading books, but for the last six of those years I've been right here, twenty minutes from your house. So how come you didn't meet me before? Something was building up in you; there was a fire burning inside and when it got to a certain point, then you found me, just down the road, waiting six years for you. It was the same for me. I had two teachers, and when I was ready, in a very magical way, they just appeared.

If I pass your test then you'll be happy to continue. If I fail your test, then you should go and look for another person. Not really look for, but you just have to be available. You may not get the teacher that you had been planning to have, he might not be perfect enough, he might not meet your ideas about how a teacher should behave, but you feel a deep connection. So even though the mind may be judging him or her as not meeting your standard, inside there is a knowing that this is the person. It is very mysterious how this connection happens.

You came here because you had a sense that I understand something that could help you end your search. It is exactly the same reason why I went to my spiritual teachers. I was touched by what they were saying and felt they could show me something. The first teacher completely changed my life because he opened up all kinds of doors and windows that I didn't even know existed.

I was able to trust him, and so when I went to the second teacher I was also able to trust him. If you yourself don't have a clear picture, that's exactly the moment when you have to trust the person you've come to get help from – because they do have a clear picture.

During the first two or three weeks I was with Papaji, I didn't understand exactly what I was supposed to see. I had lots of wrong ideas, actually, but as I'd already spent fifteen years trying to work it out myself, by that time I thought, 'Okay, lay it at his feet.' Then I could just be there and something could happen. It's a lot about trust. If you can't trust, you won't get any benefit.

I think each person has a character. Would you say that each teacher also has a character, their way of teaching?

Every teacher has a different kind of personality, a different flavour or facet, but each is communicating the same Truth. So in that way it doesn't make so much difference who your teacher is. He's just ringing the bell. But it needs to be somebody who rings the bell from emptiness. Nothingness. Somebody who knows.

Are you suggesting I don't have to take the search for a teacher so seriously?

Yes. It's a great joke actually, because you're coming here very seriously to be taught who you are. If you look at it, it's very funny, isn't it? When you finally find out who you are, you discover that who you are is who you've always been, and you're going to laugh for two days. So I might as well prepare you for the joke.

Supporting Self Awareness

It is only a very small group of people who do question and become seekers of Truth. They find themselves attracted to different teachers, different teachings and to different paths. Some of them find Truth, but many get lost along the way. I am of the strong opinion that a teacher is essential. I don't know how people are drawn to this, but I can only use the word grace. In some people's lives, grace is working to bring them to a teacher.

When I was thirty I would say I was completely lost. I was intelligent enough and educated enough – I was like an ordinarily successful guy, functioning as an architect – but in another way I was completely stupid. I didn't really understand very much on a deeper level. I had a question that had to be answered, so you could say that I never had a choice but to be a seeker.

I had two teachers in my life, and how I met them was completely mysterious. It happened despite any idea I had about it. I can see that something else was working in my life, because when it happened the first time I didn't even know what a teacher was, and I certainly wasn't looking for one. Then later I understood a lot more, but I didn't have any idea that I needed a second teacher. It seems in both those meetings I was somehow ready, even if I didn't know it myself. Completely mysterious. I was definitely in the hands of grace.

When your longing has become strong enough you will be ready to meet the teacher. When you sit in the presence of such a being it is the power of the Self coming through that person that makes you progress. Then when you are there with the teacher the best thing is to do nothing. Not nothing exactly, but to be receptive.

> *A man seeking spiritual enlightenment had been trekking across deserts and hiking over mountain ranges in the search of a particular hermit guru, renowned for his wisdom. At the peak of an icy mountain, the exhausted man found a small cave where a small man sat quietly, dressed only in rags. The man fell at the guru's feet and cried, 'Oh Guru, I have questions and I need answers. Can you help me?'*

> *'Yes,' the guru replied. He reached into his rags and pulled something out, which he then put in the seeker's hand.*
> *'What's this?'*
> *'My library card.'*

The western mind is absolutely conditioned to do, and so we think we must do a lot for anything worthwhile. If you are receptive, and if it's your turn on the list of grace, it will simply happen.

Some people have the idea that if you become involved with a spiritual teacher you are surrendering to a human being, making yourself less and therefore susceptible to an abusive situation. A true teacher would never work in that way. A true teacher wants you to realise that you are the Self! He is the Self and you are the Self. We are all the Self! The whole effort of the teacher is to bring you out of your ignorance to clarity about who you are.

During my interviews with Indian teachers for my book and film, *Blueprints for Awakening – Indian Masters*, I spoke with Swami Dayananda, a hugely respected Vedanta teacher. He was very clear on the role of the teacher, or the guru as they are referred to in India:

> *'The guru is not one who says I am guru, you are nobody! The guru is saying you are the whole; he's not saying I am the whole, you are nobody! Not only does he say that, but he also makes us see that. So the guru is the one who brings light, that's all! It's like a good friend – he tells where the best restaurant is. Guru is not authority. Guru is the one who makes you see that you're not any different from the guru.'*

When Dayananda says 'the best restaurant' he means that the guru wants to show you where *you* are and how delicious the food is there. That's all. So the teacher's role is to be a constant reminder: 'I am the Self and you are the Self. We are no different.'

In society the reminder is always to the story that you are somebody and I am somebody. The teacher's reminder is that there isn't anybody. If you bring your psychological wounds into this

Supporting Self Awareness

meeting and become resistant to the teacher there is no chance for anything to happen.

While you play that game you cut yourself off from the real guidance of the teacher. He's saying, 'I'd like to tell you where there's a wonderful restaurant,' and you're saying, 'I don't want anybody telling me where the restaurant is. I will find it myself!'

Meeting the teacher is very subtle, there is something that happens inside, a little bit like when you fall in love. Usually it is an unlikely meeting, where you suddenly find yourself feeling a strong chemistry with another. You can't help it, it just happens. It happens out of the blue and it's completely surprising. When you meet you feel 'Wow!' Then your mother says, 'Are you sure she's suitable?' But you are way beyond suitable – it has completely happened!

This is how we fall in love in a traditional way. It is the same when you meet your teacher; it just happens. Something is deeply touched when you meet and you find it hard to explain what that is.

The meeting with the teacher is deep; you just know. Then the challenge is 'Can I surrender? Can I trust this person?' Only when the surrender and trust are deep enough can the real work start.

So, if possible, be part of a spiritual group or community, have a spiritual teacher who will encourage you to become quiet and look inside, to recognise your conditioned mind and how you are so attached to 'my story'. Being in the Satsang of a true spiritual teacher – and by true I mean someone who has realised the Self – you can't escape seeing.

To become free it is important to have someone who can really see your story and reflect it back to you. It's only this illusion that you've created that prevents you from awakening. The whole effort of the teacher is to create some mechanism for you to see that, and once you do, it's all finished.

Passing on the Flame
Being With an Awakened Teacher

There's no doubt about it – if you really long for Truth then the very best advice is to spend as much time as possible with your teacher. Take them for lunch, wash their clothes and find any possible way to be with them. If this is not possible, visit your teacher at regular enough intervals that he's always there inside you. Then when you think of him, whatever the question, whatever the situation, the answer comes. By remembering the teacher you are actually remembering your own true nature.

I didn't take my teacher for lunch or wash his clothes, because other people were doing that, but after I had been with him for about three months I had a meeting with him. I was planning to bring my belongings and live nearby and in the course of this meeting he said to me, 'Very good, very good. Get your things and come back, then you can make a guesthouse for my people.'

That's what he asked me to do and so I did it, for more than four years. Every night I would be in the guesthouse as the host for dinner, and every day I would take care of the guests and organise everything that needed to be taken care of.

It wasn't an easy job, and many strong issues that lay unresolved or hidden came up to the surface in this intensive environment. It became a laboratory for me to see what was happening inside, because everybody who stepped into the guesthouse came with some kind of lesson or message for me. I don't know what my teacher's intention was, but the result was I saw many of the structures of my mind, and slowly but surely became free of them.

When it was difficult or challenging I had to let go into the trust that the situation had been provided by my teacher and that it was

Supporting Self Awareness

working in a way that perhaps I couldn't see. You could say I had to bow down to the situation, to what life, through my teacher, was bringing me. Bowing down means letting go into this relationship with the teacher, surrendering into it, and embracing whatever comes into your life as a result.

In western cultures, surrender has an overtone of defeat – surrendering to the victorious. The surrender I'm talking about in regard to a spiritual teacher is not giving up or giving in as a sign of weakness. It is realising that when I surrender to the teacher I am also surrendering to my highest Self. It's not actually surrendering to somebody, but rather to the absence of somebody.

You could see it like a brightly burning candle flame, and in front are many other candles waiting to be ignited. When the right moment comes, then simply by itself this flame ignites another candle and the light is passed on. So nobody is really doing anything.

The meeting of the disciple and the teacher comes out of a deep destiny and the workings of grace. You come and sit with a teacher and if you are surrendered and receptive then the light is passed on. The teacher doesn't do anything and the disciple doesn't do anything, so it's completly not personal. This meeting is very profound and acts beyond the understanding of the mind.

The Self of the teacher and your Self is the same Self. On a deeper level, letting go into this relationship means letting go into your true nature. This is such an important topic for everyone to understand. In the deep meeting between the teacher and the student the possibility is that you realise you are no different from the teacher. What really happens is not that you meet the teacher, it's really that you meet yourself. It's not possible for anyone's mind to ever understand this. You can't figure it out; you can only experience it, and that's the mystery.

The challenge in being with a teacher is that you will be told things you don't want to hear, or can't hear. There are different levels of hearing. Usually it starts with 'can't hear', and gradually it comes to 'hear' and then 'really hear'. To really hear is actually very rare, because usually when we hear something we bring in our own belief structure and we immediately make a judgment. If it doesn't fit with what we already believe, then we can't really hear it and we throw it away. So it's actually quite rare to really let somebody in, and that's one of the reasons why the relationship between the teacher and the student often goes on for some years. The teacher has to be very patient until the student is ready and able to hear.

> *A man's car stalled on a country road one morning. When the man got out to fix it, a cow came along and stopped beside him. 'Your trouble is probably in the carburetor,' said the cow.*
> *Startled, the man jumped back and ran down the road until he met a farmer. The amazed man told the farmer his story.*
> *'Was it a large red cow with a brown spot over the right eye?' asked the farmer.*
> *'Yes, yes,' the man replied.*
> *'Oh! I wouldn't listen to Bessie,' said the farmer. 'She doesn't know a thing about cars.'*

The teacher doesn't actually have much to say, but he has to wait until he can pop a few words into the letterbox. Obviously, to pop something in the letterbox it has to be open. Most letterboxes are locked shut. First you have to be able to hear, and then you have to understand the message. You can't really know when you've misinterpreted the message; you just have to trust the inner process. Anyway, we often misunderstand. It can't be helped. You can only do what you can do. I wouldn't worry about all that – it'll just happen how it happens.

Words can be interpreted in many different ways. As I said, usually when you hear something you bring out all your beliefs and immediately reject it. So it doesn't even matter if it's in your own language or not. The more essential point is whether there's openness, whether the heart is really open and whether there is some trust. Later there may be surrender, but it all happens by itself; you can't really do any of these things.

Supporting Self Awareness

There has to be a really open-hearted connection between the teacher and the student because the teacher's task of taking away the ego will always come to a painful moment. He can do a few fillings; he can polish your teeth. It's all quite nice, but there are going to be a few rotten old teeth he has to pull out, and that is always going to be painful. A nice teacher who always keeps you feeling really good is not necessarily doing a good job because part of his work is to challenge the ego, that which prevents you simply living in the Self.

All our nice, comfortable little attachments will have to go. Naturally, some of them are held onto very tightly. It is bound to be painful. There is no way to really avoid that. You will want to run away many times. It is not that the teacher suddenly gives you some information and you say, 'Wow! That's it!' It is more like he blocks all your escape routes. If you actually leave then that is really a big waste because even if you run away to another teacher, at some point, if he is any good, he will bring you to the same place that you ran away from.

Projection and resistance to authority, particularly to male authority, are common occurrences for a student with a teacher. It's always frustrating when the teacher is projected onto as 'somebody'. You make him somebody and then you resist that somebody, without seeing that you first of all created him and then resisted him. This is a useless game!

In our community, the most dramatic in this resistance to authority are the men, and very often they have strong disagreements, and even leave in resistance to me. Over the years, I've taken on the role of decision maker in the community, and even though I am happy to give away this role, it very often comes back to me. So I have become a kind of authority.

As a beautiful example of this I want to tell you about Mario, a Portuguese man with a strong desire to become free and a natural understanding of this possibility. It's always been difficult for him to trust and it's always been difficult for him to deal with male authority. So although we have a deep connection, he always has the sense that he can't communicate with me. After a retreat weekend where he had faced a strong personal issue with authority, he was part of a meeting of the main organisers of the community. During this meeting there was a sudden explosion of resistance from him when I suggested he move his mountain bike out of the community store room and put it with all the other bikes. It was seemingly a small thing, but it pushed his buttons so fiercely that he jumped up in anger and rushed out of the room.

Next morning he had packed all his belongings in his car and was determined to head back to Portugal. He was absolutely clear that he would drive off, and he wasn't open in the beginning to hear anything. That changed after a talk with some of the heartful ladies of the community. Later I arranged to meet him in the garden and go into his issue.

Everything has been building up for three weeks. Do you remember the meeting we had where I realised I was not coming to the meditations because I was proud and arrogant?

You realised you weren't coming to the meditations because you thought I wanted you to come?

Yes, it was my way of sending the message to the authority that I will do what I want. Anyway, everything built up to a climax and after my explosion at the meeting yesterday I basically saw the misunderstanding about my life. I saw that vulnerability isn't about weakness; it's about inner strength.

Male children are not encouraged to be vulnerable.

I felt an enormous fear and I wanted to be finished with it. At some point I realised that allowing vulnerability is a kind of inner strength, especially in the face of something like resistance to male authority.

Supporting Self Awareness

Yes, being vulnerable is actually just an invitation to be as you are. There seems to be more pressure in this area on men than on women. The male ego cannot appear weak. It's quite subtle, but being who you are doesn't include teenage rebellion. That's part of the game of resistance.

The mature way to deal with male authority is not to care about it but to get on with your life. The message of this whole story is to be as you are, not as Mummy or Daddy wanted you to be as a little boy.

He didn't drive off to Portugal, and that evening, when he was alone in his room, he had a glimpse of the Self. After his resistance and the decision to leave and then to stay, it was clear things would be working inside him. I was prepared to support him the next day when he came to share his experience in a public meeting.

I was aware of a lot of amazing things last night. All of a sudden the moments of pain and resistance transformed into wonderful sensations and warmth.

Are you saying that when you were resistant you felt cold, but when you became open you felt rather warm?

Yes, as if a lot of energy suddenly moved after holding on to it for a long time. I was aware for the first time of my ideas passing by and me laughing and crying at the same time about them. I know they will come again because it's not grounded or settled.

But the difference will be that you now have a new understanding.

That's the funny part. I've read about resistance, but it's so different when it happens directly. The understanding doesn't come from speaking about it and 'feeling' is also not really the right word.

It's more like knowing at a deep level, whereas before you understood from an intellectual position. Welcome to the rest of your life! It could be very different now. Everybody who knows you can see the stiffness has gone from your face.

This morning my face was almost painful from the energy moving through me.

Yes! It's painful to relax. This is such a beautiful example of resistance turning into something completely unexpected. As soon as you decided to stay and not run away, there was an enormous energy available. Then last night that energy manifested and it shifted something strongly in you.

Resistance offers a possibility, a beautiful possibility, because as you become resistant to a situation or to a person the energy builds up inside you. In moments of greatest resistance towards the teacher there is the possibility of the greatest clarity and understanding. As soon as you have a major issue with the teacher you can be sure, without even one word being spoken, that you are wrong.

When your expectations of how a teacher should behave are not met, you have two choices. You can get caught up in your thoughts and judgments or you can watch your mind at work. Your awareness is always about you; it is never about the teacher. As soon as you have an issue with something or someone on the outside then you are already lost, because in the end everything has to be brought back to yourself. If the teacher has provoked you into resistance over a powerful issue, something that you don't want to recognise, something that you don't want to see, something that seems to be too terrifying, it is much easier to blame the teacher than to look in the mirror that the situation offers. There is an enormous energy locked up in that resistant moment, and if it is released through a new understanding it works for you instead of against you.

Supporting Self Awareness

If in the future you experience what I am talking about, it is a wonderful moment to have the courage to step forward and ask the teacher to help you with what is happening. It is one of the most profound moments to ask for help, and out of that help you can have clarity of understanding on which to make your decision, on which to understand what is really happening at a deeper level.

> *Prince Gautama, who had become Buddha, saw one of his followers meditating under a tree at the edge of the Ganges. Upon enquiring why he was meditating, his follower stated that he was attempting to become so enlightened he could cross the river unaided. Buddha gave him a few rupees and said: 'Why don't you seek passage with that boatman? It is much easier.'*

Every time you get a big hit from the teacher it doesn't help you to run away and say, 'Anyway, he was a terrible teacher. I was really lucky to get away from him.' The right response is, 'Thank you very much for that hit. Please hit me harder next time.'

Trust or devotion is very important because this bond of love, this open-hearted connection, includes a tremendous energetic support for going through very difficult moments. If you really want to become free, the work is not finished at the moment of Self-realisation. The spiritual work continues, cleaning up everything, particularly the conditioned mind. For that the teacher is very valuable because he has an insight into your false self.

Resistance is never about this or that issue. It is always about your understanding and your commitment to becoming free. The issue is simply a chance to let go and remain in that deeper place that is not cluttered with everything you think you know. Unfortunately, what often happens when resistance arises is that people just leave the situation. At a certain point the teacher will see you, he will know you and know what is between you and freedom. Then he will do something to create a situation, provoking you in some way.

You will become resistant, and he knows this. Teachers know

that if they make you pissed off, then something is happening. Teachers would like you to be in true peace, of course, but they don't particularly want everything to be peaceful. There's always a storm around the teacher because he's acting as a strong mirror.

It's a strange paradox that people come to a teacher wanting life to become peaceful but then they look around and see everyone around the teacher is far from peaceful. They say, 'Well, that's a bit funny! He can't be a very good teacher, because look at them all!' But actually, it's not like that. You have to understand the dynamic that's going on. When you are truly peaceful, nothing can disturb that peace. What the teacher does is act as a catalyst to show you where you are not yet peaceful, to show you what's causing the disturbance. If you become truly peaceful, whatever the teacher would do or say will never take you away from that peace.

As I see it, if a student runs away while in strong resistance it's a great opportunity missed. If you stay there, in this resistance, working with it, there can be a powerful movement and a great opening can happen.

> *The master of the house is comfortably seated in an armchair in the library, reading a newspaper. Suddenly, John, his butler, rips the door open and shouts, 'Sir, the River Thames is flooding the streets!'*
> *The master looks up calmly from the newspaper and says, 'John, please. I have already told you before, if you do have something important to tell me, first knock on the door then enter and inform me, in a quiet and civilised manner, about the issue. Now please, do so.'*
> *John apologises and closes the door behind him. Three seconds later, the master hears a knock on the door. 'Yes?'*
> *John partially enters the room and with a sweeping gesture he announces, 'Sir, the Thames.'*

You absolutely have to trust the workings of destiny and accept the grace of the meeting. The teacher knows something that you want to

Supporting Self Awareness

know, and his whole effort is to help you with that. He sees the right moment in which to do a little trick, different for each individual, and in that moment you realise you are the same as the teacher. Then it's all over. This is his only interest.

Chapter 2
Supporting Self Awareness

*In Satsang we become quiet,
we leave our stories and dramas behind
and we come to stillness.
We are that stillness.
It's absolutely beautiful
because it's so incredibly simple.
It's a complete turn around.
You don't need anything from the outside.
You've got it all there, everything.
Satsang is a reminder of who we are,
and who we are is always here.*

Chapter 2
Supporting Self Awareness

How much effort do we put into trying to change our lives to become more happy and content? It is not about changing anything. It is about becoming aware of what is, stepping back from our habit of separation, quietening the busy mind and becoming a witness to our lives. Spiritual practices such as meditation and Yoga – alone or with a group – support this awareness, and there can also be a powerful support in meeting and working with a spiritual teacher.

Moving to Silence 33
Meditation and Self-Awareness

Stepping Towards Grace 40
Associating With Truth

Seeking the Light 47
Finding a Guide to Awakening

Passing on the Flame 53
Being With an Awakened Teacher

beginner, join a meditation circle or group. When you first start, it's not always easy to meditate alone. We are so used to being both physically and mentally active and a group can support and encourage a regular practice. It's helpful also to have a meditation teacher who can guide you.

> *Two men meet on the street.*
> *One asks the other: 'Hi, how are you?'*
> *The other one replies: 'I'm fine, thanks.'*
> *'And how's your son? Is he still unemployed?'*
> *'Yes, he is. But he is meditating now.*
> *'Meditating? What's that?'*
> *'I don't know. But it's better than sitting around and doing nothing!'*

By meditating regularly you can develop a quieter mind, by which I mean a mind that is not busy, not churning up as many thoughts and distractions as normal, and not creating a kind of background buzz or fog in your life that prevents you from being clear. A quiet mind is an important foundation for awareness because it allows you to look more deeply inside yourself. Once you get the hang of it, then you can bring it into your daily life more and more easily.

There are many forms of meditation ranging from Zazen or Vipassana to simply focusing on a candle flame or on your breath. A regular practice creates some effect after quite a short time. This could be anything from feeling more peaceful to a strengthened immune system. The greatest benefits of meditation are that you learn self-awareness and silence.

In the community we practise meditation every morning and again at lunchtime, and we sit together in silence to eat dinner. The point of the morning meditation is to come to stillness. The day passes with more space inside and we find ourselves less stressed, more open, more relaxed and more in a flow with ourselves and with life. We also practise Yoga each morning because many structures are held also in our bodies. Yoga can help unlock some of these structures.

Moving to Silence
Meditation and Self Awareness

Where I live in Germany is very close to several motorways. I often drive there, enjoying the untamed speed limit and appreciating the many beautiful cars you seem to see everywhere in Germany. One particular day I was driving to a meeting in Cologne when suddenly one of my front tires blew out and I had to swerve out of the fast lanes and pull slowly off to the side. It had happened before so I wasn't particularly bothered by the incident. I called a repair service and settled down by the side of the busy highway to wait.

Outside of the car you really get a different sense of the pace of life on a motorway. The cars look more like rockets, and the ground shakes continuously as they roar past. What is everyone so frantically rushing towards? What are we searching for? Is it for money, for happiness or particularly for love? Perhaps we imagine love lies at the end of the motorway, or is the whole rush just a movement towards happiness? These are the questions that trigger the spiritual search for many people as they begin to look at what life is really about.

A fruitful place to begin answering these questions is to look at how strongly your thoughts are pulling you into the search for love and happiness out there in the world. Sit by the side of the motorway of your life for a while and watch how you rush. Watch what ideas are pulling you ever onwards and outwards.

Examining these ideas will show you what is driving you and one of the most useful tools in this examination is silence. Learn to become quiet. If you are new to this then probably the first step is a spiritual practice, such as meditation, breath work or mantra singing. I would personally recommend meditation. If you're a

Chapter 3
What is Real? Life is About Waking Up

*There must be a reason why everyone has an ego.
Perhaps it is a little joke from existence.
By first acquiring and then recognising it,
you have the opportunity to consciously drop it.
Stepping out of the ego,
you consciously know 'that's not who I am'.
When there is no identification with the ego
you go back to your natural state,
like a two-year-old.
The difference is
that now you are conscious of it.*

Chapter 3
What is Real? Life is About Waking Up

Even with deeper awareness, we often still feel a strong sense of separation. We can ask ourselves why we have this sense of separation. Why do we struggle? What is in the way of happiness? What is the meaning of our lives? If we are not the body then who are we, and what is death? The answer to all these questions comes back to the same fundamental message – wake up to who you really are and see that nothing is separate.

Garden of Eden 65
Ego and Struggle

The Price of Happiness 72
The Fear of Survival

Dying into Whiteness 79
The Fear of Death

Be As You Are 86
Living Our True Nature

The World 92
Our Mistaken Ideas

Garden of Eden
Ego and Struggle

We live by a large green park that borders the river and attracts the whole village when the weather is good. There is a playground at the centre of this lovely park, where a hub of youthful activity usually happens.

The children run around, meeting, playing, laughing, crying, fighting, falling, jumping. It's constant movement, and so beautifully fresh. The children are naturally present. One may fall from the slide and burst into tears, but after a brushing down and a kiss from mum, the child is sprinting back with his friends to the next adventure, his cheeks still wet from the tears, but the pain itself completely disappeared from his memory.

It is a gift to sit amidst this flow of innocence and presence, and I have encouraged people living with me to go to this very playground and observe the children. What can they teach you? Innocence, presence and causeless joy. Children are spontaneous and fearless. These are the qualities of your essential nature.

> *A priest is walking down the street one day when he notices a very small boy trying to press a doorbell on a house across the street. However, the boy is very small and the doorbell is too high for him to reach.*
> *After watching the boy's efforts for some time, the priest steps quickly across the street, walks up behind the little fellow and placing his hand kindly on the child's shoulder leans over and gives the doorbell a good ring.*
> *Crouching down to the child's level, the priest smiles benevolently and asks, 'And now what, my little man?'*
> *To which the boy replies, 'Now we run!'*

What is Real? Life is About Waking Up

The qualities of innocence and joy so easily lived in childhood are covered over as the ego develops. This question of what covers our natural, child-like innocence was put to me recently by Lin, a community resident. She was watching the children playing with one of the parrots that we keep as part of the community zoo. The parrot was hopping on the table and the children were laughing at its antics. Lin was touched by the joy in that moment, and clearly felt a strong sense of missing it in her daily life.

―――

These kids are so spontaneous and present. Why do we grow out of this and into ego? Watching them playing and seeing the simple joy on their faces triggers joy in me. Usually I see everything through a filter of 'me', and it's not joyful at all.

We adults get lost in the idea of being separate. Why does that happen? Why not always live in Truth? As babies we don't have much sense of ego. In the beginning, a baby doesn't feel any separation between himself and his mother. Then, as he learns that everyone and everything has a name that distinguishes it from everything else, this sense of separation gradually increases. Slowly he develops an ego. It happens in a natural way. As the sense of separation leads to the formation of an ego, so the identification with a false self develops, which inevitably leads to suffering.

Eventually, our desire to be free from this suffering causes us to try and understand it. We can investigate the nature of the ego by becoming quiet and looking inward. When it is finally revealed as false it disappears, bringing us back to our original nature. We are back in the Garden of Eden. But now there is a difference because there is consciousness. As little children we have no ego, but we don't know that; we are not conscious. We have to go out of the Garden of Eden in order to understand it. We can say the ego gives us an opportunity to develop consciousness.

Garden of Eden

If I understand correctly, ego is like a teacher?

Yes. You could say it like that. It could be that the point of human life is simply to become free and that life itself is set up as a vast laboratory to help you. Instead of seeing your daughter playing happily and thinking, 'She is so joyful and I am not,' you can see it as a reminder from life that you are not currently living that. You are reminded of your sense of separation and you can take the opportunity to become aware of it. Then going out of the Garden of Eden and finding your way back can be the ultimate reason for your life.

The reason being that I find the Self?

Yes, you will find the Self. Not *your* Self, but *the* Self. We are all actually perfect as we are, even if we are lost. It's totally alright to be lost. Living life from moment to moment as it unfolds gives us an opportunity to become clear and conscious.

It seems that as human beings we have to go from innocence and clarity as young children into confusion and addictive conditioning, apparent separateness, pain and suffering. As human beings we also have the qualities that can take us out of that. When we become free we know who we are consciously, which is what a child doesn't know.

Every evening we have a meditation period that includes eating dinner together in silence. It is a time to become still and quiet, following a busy day. We sit together around a huge table, enjoying the food and the silence. When everybody has finished eating we sit without doing anything for five or ten minutes. Gradually a beautiful feeling of nothing arises. It is very profound, and within the emptiness there is a sense of sitting with old friends, with everybody and with everything.

There is no energy from anyone to ask 'How was your day?

What is Real? Life is About Waking Up

What did you think of this or that? Did you watch the football?' It is nothing like that; just silence. There is a nourishing pool of emptiness, and you melt inside.

In this space my conversation with Lin came to mind, especially her earnest question about the meaning of life and why we have an ego. My answer from this space would be, 'Who cares?' It is completely unimportant. On some deeper level you know that life will take care of itself; life goes on, and you don't have to worry about it. You can just be here now in this emptiness.

The whole point of life, you could say, or of having an ego, is to go through this struggle and to finally become clear. Over many years I have grown up believing that I am my thoughts, I am my body, I am my feelings, and out of this I have constructed 'me', my ego. If you investigate for yourself you can't find this 'me', yet with every experience in your life you refer back to it. 'I think this. I believe that. I know this. I like this. I prefer that. I judge this situation to be like that.' Everything is referred back to 'I', with the assumption that there is an 'I', an ego, and that this is who we are.

When we're two years old we don't have much of an ego. We're not really identified and we feel one with everything. Gradually we get a sense of ourselves as separate from everything and everyone else, and by the time we are adults we're completely locked into a false idea of who we are, which we absolutely believe – 'me', 'I'. This little 'I' is exactly the great misunderstanding. It is very difficult to see it, but as soon as you do there is a deconstruction of the false self and a recognition of your true nature. The identification with a separate somebody drops. It happens automatically; you don't have to do anything. The whole system gets shaken up suddenly and wants to find harmony again.

Lin asked, 'Why do we have an ego? What's the point of it?' You may have noticed that everybody has one. It's pretty rare to meet someone who doesn't. Village people who still live in harmony with nature and with themselves can have these child-like qualities of innocence and spontaneity, but probably they don't know themselves consciously.

Garden of Eden

A kindergarten teacher was observing her classroom of children while they drew. She would occasionally walk around to see each child's artwork. As she got to one little girl who was working diligently, she asked what the drawing was.
The girl replied, 'I'm drawing God.'
The teacher paused and said, 'But no one knows what God looks like.'
Without missing a beat or looking up from her drawing the girl replied, 'They will in a minute.'

There must be a reason why everyone has an ego. Perhaps it is a little joke from existence. By first acquiring and then recognising it, you have the opportunity to consciously drop it. Stepping out of the ego, you consciously know 'that's not who I am'. When there is no identification with the ego you go back to your natural state, that of a two-year-old. The difference is that now you are conscious of it.

You were conscious of being separate and now are conscious of the opposite. It's a very beautiful and completely natural way to live. If you're pissed off, you're pissed off; if you're happy, you're happy. Food tastes good, you're happy; food tastes bad, you're also okay, because nothing matters anymore.

That's why I can say, 'Who cares about the answer to the question?' You have to find out who it is that asks the question. Who are you really identified with? Is that really you? Is that who you are, the one that has been constructed over the years of your development as a human being?

We are in the habit of bringing everything that happens in our life back to this 'I'. When you see that this construction of 'me', 'my story', 'I', is not real, then it will let you go. You can begin to live from your being; the whole quality of your life will change. It seems you need this false story, this misidentification, just to realise that it is not the reality.

The mind has been conditioned to believe that 'I' must do something so that I can have my lunch, pay my rent and buy my new car. I must make my life happy. This is the mind talking. Actually, existence is doing the work – without any help from you. The whole universe is the manifestation of consciousness.

We often talk about a spiritual journey, but there's nowhere to go to and there's nothing to find. It's already all here. We are already exactly as we should be. We all believe we are making our life happen, but in fact when we become quiet we find that the Self is just happening and we will always be taken care of. We will have the experiences we need in life to learn the lessons we need to learn and we will be supported by existence.

I would say the ultimate support in seeing through the misunderstanding of who you are is a teacher, someone who has been through the same process and can act as a catalyst for you becoming clear, helping to guide you from the suffering of identification into freedom. Here is a story, set in a small village, that illustrates this.

The village people were having trouble with a lion that was taking their livestock. They decided to hunt the lion and kill it, but they didn't notice that it had a cub. The little cub was left alone in the bushes, and, having lost his mother, became rather lonely. At that point a flock of sheep passed by, found the young lion and took him along with them. Naturally, after some time this lion cub was eating grass and going 'baahhh', just like the sheep.

The little lion grew bigger and bigger, living very happily with the sheep. In fact, he thought he was a sheep. Every day he would eat grass and go 'baahhh'. Things continued like this for some time until one day an old wise lion was passing by, looking for something nice to eat. He started moving down towards the sheep when, to his surprise, in the middle of the flock he saw a lion. The lion was eating grass and going 'baahhh', just like a sheep.

The old lion made a move towards the young lion, terrifying the whole flock. He grabbed the young lion and dragged him, kicking and baahhh-ing in terror, right down to the edge of the lake. The young lion still thought he was a sheep being taken away by a hungry lion. The lake was very calm, and when the young lion looked into the surface of the water and saw his reflection he was very surprised to see that he looked just like the wise old lion. Suddenly, in that moment, he realised that he was a lion. And he roared!

Find out who you are and roar your roar, dance your dance. The divine Absolute is the essence of every human being, of all the birds and animals, the rocks and trees and of the whole planet and the entire universe. We are also ordinary men and woman, and this interface between our ordinariness and our divine nature is the essence of our misunderstanding.

The Price of Happiness
The Fear of Survival

When I arrived in Germany seven years ago I had a suitcase, the clothes on my back and minus five thousand euro in my bank account. I also didn't know anyone. It could have been seen as a slightly hopeless situation, and one where trust in life could have been an issue. However, it was such an exciting time because everything just unfolded from there and I found myself meeting people, travelling and always having the money and support I needed to survive and flourish.

I left my career as an architect when I was twenty-seven and I've never had a conventional job since. Sometimes it has been tough, sometimes abundant. I can say that I frequently had a fear of not surviving – often triggered by the lack of money – that created suffering in my life. I eventually realised that the amount of energy spent in this suffering was completely sabotaging any real inner contentment and happiness.

Nowadays, I live in the trust that my means for living will always be provided. I am not preoccupied with it and this gives a great space just to enjoy the life that is unfolding.

I travelled to Brussels recently, as I had been invited to give Satsang. Through the people I met I noticed the power that money had in their society and how its importance was constantly stressed in people's lives.

One man I spoke with worked many hours a week as a fairly high-powered diplomat in the centre of town. A couple of years before, he had burnt out from the sheer quantity of work on his plate. The levels of stress had built up until he couldn't manage anymore. During his recovery he was shocked at how his life had been – caught

The Price of Happiness

up endlessly in stress and overload – and he discovered meditation. He lived quietly for some time, but for some reason he then took his old job back, working much less than he had previously, but again in a fairly stressful environment.

He didn't forget his connection to meditation and self-reflection, and through his practice and enquiry he was attracted to come to my Satsang meeting.

I simply want to be what I am, but I am afraid I would have no control over my survival.

What does that mean?

My life is full of deadlines and meetings, and if I withdraw from that and just be how I am, I feel my life would have many new difficulties.

Best to stay then. Just stay there in all those deadlines and meetings. Much better. Who made all these deadlines? Are they written somewhere?

No, but I can't just leave it all behind. It is necessary for my survival.

Do you see that through this attempt to survive, almost everything in your life – especially working in a city in a job like yours – is slanted in some way towards merchandise and deadlines?

I didn't say that it's a better way to live, but I'm living here, in this life, here on this earth, and I have to earn money and secure my future. I have to pay my rent. I have a tax number. It seems I can't just drop all that.

I know that you were involved in meditation after your burn-out, and at times you probably discovered something inside you that was untouched by what was happening on the outside. Is that right?

What is Real? Life is About Waking Up

Yes, there were clear, very beautiful moments when it felt like everything was already taken care of. It was very deep, but it gets so covered up by the demands of daily life.

If you come into a deep understanding of who you really are – which you have had some insight into – then you are in your essential nature. You are simply present and part of this cosmos, this phenomenon we call consciousness.

Is there any value then in accumulating money or putting effort into creating security for the future?

There is tremendous pressure on people to devote their lives to accumulating money and putting it into safe investments, which will supposedly give them eternal life!

Of course, having a job that provides money for living is one way that existence takes care of you. Become present with what you are doing and relax about the future. There will always be enough. There is a profound connectedness, and in this there is a bountiful support for our daily needs.

This enormous focus on accumulating money is completely false. There is a sense that if you have a lot of money your life must be happy and if you are very poor then your life must be very unhappy. But my personal experience is that it is simply not true.

How can I live when I am in this state of nothing?

Ah! That's a good question. You don't have to do anything. It all works by itself. While you are busy paying the rent, life is happening anyway. Have you ever thought how that happens? The sun comes out, the rain falls, the rice grows, babies are born and people die. It's all just happening. While you think you are doing it, it's happening, and if you stop 'doing your life' it will absolutely still happen. While you are busy thinking 'I am doing my life', life is just unfolding.

The Price of Happiness

Great! God did a great job! He deserves Sundays off! While you try to *do* your life, you can never *be*.

It's just happening?

Yes! How could I have planned our meeting? We had to meet, you see? I came to Brussels, you were here and we were destined to meet here tonight.

• ——— •

Much of life has become solely focused on material wealth. Money has become the focus all around the world, and through that focus the planet itself has become threatened by the ecological consequences. Yet the economic rationalism of the planet always takes first place. The needs of the planet in terms of population and ecological balance always come second, even though in the last three or four decades there has been ever-increasing awareness of ecological damage.

As far as I can see, this whole chase for money, goods and survival comes from two basic ideas: we want to be happy, and we think we are a body that needs to survive. We all want happiness, but we think we can get it from a good bottle of beer, a glass of wine, a new partner, our soul mate or a bit more money.

Do these things really make us happy? Maybe for a short time there is enjoyment from getting something materialistic: 'Oh, what a great holiday! I am definitely a bit happier.' Hoping something on the outside will make us happy is a hook we human beings have invented for ourselves, always keeping us dependent on new desires.

But it is simply not possible for real happiness to come from the outside. Think how beautiful that is. It means that you can find it right now because you already have it. If you would just stop, you would find it. It's just there, waiting for you, and all efforts to find it elsewhere take you further away.

Money in its essence is fine; it is a tool that humanity has invented, but it has become an obsession out of this fear that we will not survive. The fact is we are all *not* going to survive. If you see yourself as just the body, you are not going to survive. If you see yourself as the eternal Self then you are here eternally, forever and ever. The eternal Self is a never-changing, absolutely constant phenomenon.

This essential part of our nature is absolutely untouched by issues of survival. If we come into a deep understanding of the eternal Self then death and birth don't exist. In presence, in consciousness, there is nowhere to go and nothing to acquire.

We are happiness itself, and it doesn't cost anything. It is all completely given. Existence always takes care of us, even though our understanding is, 'I have to do my life, and if I don't do my life it's not going to work.' It may not work out the way we planned or the way we hoped, but the important thing is to be present for your life, the life that is actually happening.

We are so used to being in control, or wanting to be in control of our relationships, our jobs, our income, our entire life. It's a habit; it's all we know. The controller is the false self, the 'somebody'. When you say 'no' from this false self, you can feel the energy of contraction in your body. Saying 'yes', without wanting to change anything, is surrender to life as it is. You can feel the expansion in your body. 'Yes' allows you to dissolve into life, into what is.

This kind of acceptance is very threatening because it leads to the deconstruction of the ego. The fastest way to give it up is to say 'yes, yes, yes', even in situations where you would like to say 'no' – particularly in situations where you would like to say 'no'. This is extremely difficult because you will always come to some point where you can't say 'yes'.

These challenges present themselves every day. Most of them are quite small, but if you get in the habit and the flow of saying 'yes', you begin to live in an acceptance of what is, no matter what the situation. 'Yes' feels like a lightness or an expansion in the body. This will lead you to the happiness that is waiting inside you.

The Price of Happiness

Natural happiness is actually who we are. It is the same nature as the birds singing. When small children are playing together they feel happy when they build their sand castles on the beach and they also feel happy when the waves come and break them down as the tide comes in. It is not really complicated. This joy is natural; we just have to make contact with it. The only thing preventing this contact is all the conditioning in our minds that tells us life should be a certain way.

In the world of duality, meaning the play of two, happiness and unhappiness are absolutely connected, but you can step out of that whole game and then there is no question about it anymore. Actually there's not really happiness anymore either. There's a deep, continuous sense of nourishment or wellbeing, and that foundation is not affected by happiness or unhappiness. You don't feel better if you're happy or worse if you're unhappy. This foundation accepts everything. It is your nature, and it's very ordinary.

> *An old man is sitting in the park, crying his eyes out. A young jogger comes by and asks him what's wrong.*
> *The old man says, 'I'm a multimillionaire. I have a great big house, the fastest car in the world and I just married a beautiful blonde bombshell who satisfies me every night in bed whether I like it or not (sob sob).'*
> *The young jogger says, 'Man, you have everything I have ever dreamed of! What could be so wrong in your life that you are sitting here in the park crying?'*
> *The old man says, 'I can't remember where I live.'*

I'm almost embarrassed to say that I'm happy all the time. Even if I feel anger, sadness or pain there is an underlying ground of peace and a deep acceptance of what is. It's worse than happy; it's like 'Wow! Wow!' All the time, 'Wow!' I haven't done anything for that. It's my nature. I'm just built like that. When I arrived on this planet 'Wow!' was included, just for free. Everybody's got it, yet we have lost touch with it.

What is Real? Life is About Waking Up

A lot of people don't even know that this inner happiness exists, unfortunately, and so we have created a society based on desire and greed. A voracious advertising industry is trying to make us want things that actually we can't really afford and a huge promotional industry is trying to convince us that if we really want to be happy then we need a holiday in Barbados or a thousand other things. Without that we can't really be happy.

Like the old man on the park bench and the seeker from Brussels, we forget that we are everything we could ever want. As the world cannot give happiness, just close your eyes, look inside and discover that you are happiness itself. You've got a lot of Wow! in there. You're full of Wow! If you are not careful you can explode from so much Wow! You just burst apart!

Dying into Whiteness
The Fear of Death

There is a garden at the side of our community, which for a long time was empty and held very little appeal to anyone passing through. Over the last year we planted grass, flowers and trees, and we put out chairs and benches and a sitting circle made of large logs. It had become very beautiful, but still lacked something. It needed movement; it needed life. We decided to buy an assortment of unusual chickens that could wander round and give some character and atmosphere to the area.

As we released them into the garden, they ran for corners or buried themselves under the hay. To give them time to acclimatise we left them overnight in their chicken coop. The next day the zoo keeper opened the door to let the morning sunlight in and started to usher them towards the door, the sunlight and the green grass beyond.

After some hesitation, they all decided that outside would be a better deal than the slightly dingy, smelly interior where they had spent the night – apart from one, a little guy with feathers covering his eyes. He ran everywhere but to the door, as if he was afraid of the sunlight and the greater space beyond him. He dug himself into a corner, and had a good hold. Prodding gently, the zoo keeper slowly brought him to the door. He was finally dislodged and stepped away from the dark place where he had been hiding and padded down the ramp.

Fearing the end of the known, even if it is dark and smelly, is the most common fear for anyone journeying into themselves, and often this fear is not recognised.

For awakening to happen, there needs to be a priority and a

What is Real? Life is About Waking Up

clarity. Maybe you know the situation where something beautiful happens, or you go to Satsang and your thoughts disappear and you feel tremendous bliss and stillness and you're completely inside with yourself. Then you go home and get involved in your usual activities and relationships. When you wake up the next morning you know that the silence and bliss have disappeared and you are back in the world of 'my life'. Being really ready to wake up and step out of all this means being ready to totally surrender your life. Everything. Totally. So this is not for everybody. Actually, it is for almost nobody!

Sitting in the garden with one of the community residents, we considered the implications of this. We drank a cold juice together and talked while our new chickens pecked and scratched around us on the grass.

I feel a lot of fear of letting go. I also find that I am clinging to my ideas, my habits and the old way that I've been acting and living my life. And then, looking inside, often now I come to this empty nothing. Beautiful...but I am scared of this 'nothingness'.

In one way I want to be free of my limitations and problems, but in another sense I'm clinging to them, because they're part of my identity. I'm very connected to these habits and limitations, and I fear something like death.

You are afraid of something dying that never existed. You were never 'doing' your life. You were never running the show. That's just part of the false identification.

We feel secure in the idea of being a separate somebody, and the idea that this identification could melt away or deconstruct feels like death, something final. We're really stepping into the unknown, and that brings fear. The longing for freedom and the fear of 'death' work together.

Yes, exactly. It's amazing that I can actually watch this movement of becoming afraid, especially through examining who it is that is afraid. Seeing it opens something inside and creates some space around the fear.

As you become more aware of your story it gets really boring; it gets really old and stinking, and you know it doesn't work. You have been doing your story for so long and it never worked. It nearly always comes to the same stinking end.

You have been incredibly resistant and fearful and right now your challenge is to see that the fear is misplaced. In any moment you do not know what the next moment will bring. You fear the next moment because, on some level, you are afraid of your *last* moment. There is a fear of death, but actually what you will experience in the last moment of your life, the moment of death, is essentially no different from what you experience in every other moment.

The people you leave behind will be gnashing their teeth over your dead body, but for you, it won't be like that. So there is actually no reason to fear that moment, or to fear *this* moment. When you see that clearly, then you can go the other way and simply embrace life. You can embrace this moment, and, with great relish, be open to the next moment, knowing full well that you coped with all the moments and that you will cope with all the next moments.

So you're saying that the fear I'm experiencing is also an illusion, created by the mind?

Yes, because what is fear? It is an idea about the future. You're afraid of dying, yes? We have fear of our death in the future because we believe that now we are here. But what we think of as 'here' is, in fact, an illusion. If you believe the illusion strongly enough, then you can believe that this illusion is going to die. You become afraid because it feels like the end. But you're afraid of the death of an illusion, something that never existed.

This fear that you're talking about is a real fear, but it's based on an illusion. We believe 'we' die, as separate individuals. Facing our fear and the inevitability of the death of the body can lead us to enquiring about what is left when the body dies. When *everything* is gone, only the Self remains.

•———•

A couple made a deal that whoever died first would come back and tell the other if there is sex after death. Their biggest fear was that there was no afterlife at all. After a long life together, the husband was the first to die. True to his word, he made the first contact:
'Marion...Marion.'
'Is that you, Bob?'
'Yes, I've come back like we agreed.'
'That's wonderful! What's it like?'
'Well, I get up in the morning, I have sex, I have breakfast and then it's off to the golf course. I have sex again, bathe in the warm sun and then have sex a couple more times. Then I have lunch (you'd be proud – lots of vegetables). Another play around the golf course, then pretty much have sex the rest of the afternoon. After supper, it's back to the golf course again. Then it's more sex until late at night. I catch some much needed sleep and then the next day it starts all over again.'
'Oh, Bob, are you in Heaven?'
'No...I'm a rabbit.'

One of my favorite authors and spiritual teachers is the Russian, George Gurdjieff. In some ways he was the first of the modern masters. In his book, *Meetings with Remarkable Men*, he describes a meeting with someone who became his very dear friend. This friend had dedicated his life to finding Truth and freedom. He had searched through the whole world looking for somebody who could show him Truth, and finally he met someone who told him of a great master living in a faraway monastery. If he wanted to go there then there was a condition. He had to leave his whole life behind and never return. Symbolically, this is what is needed if you want to meet Truth.

I am not saying that you have to leave your family, your city, your work, but inside you have to be ready to give up everything. Everything that you hold on to prevents the awakening. Almost everybody wants to stay in the structures of their life. We naturally prefer to be a somebody because of the fear associated with thinking we are a nobody.

It's scary, because intrinsic to becoming a nobody is the death of the somebody. So a great fear of death can arise. We play a funny game with this fear of death, because however natural it may feel, it is irrational. It is only the illusionary false self that dissolves. This false self can't embrace God and the mystery of life. It can't let the Self unfold and surrender – after all, it might take you on a path that doesn't fit your plan. You want to be able to manage the next moment. Wanting things to be a certain way creates a huge tension inside the mind.

Every Wednesday evening in the community we celebrate with music and mantra singing, bringing everyone into a beautiful heartfulness and openness. During one of these evenings a woman had an out of body experience, a glimpse of the fact that she is not the body. She had been having strong experiences for some time and now, with the music and singing in full swing she unexpectedly and slowly fell to the floor as if unconscious, with a great smile on her face.

We checked that she was okay then left her to whatever was happening inside her. It was clearly not a physical problem, but rather that something profound in her spirit, in her energy system, had shifted.

After half an hour she slowly came out of this state and began to cry quite dramatically. Her body shook uncontrollably. No one knew what was happening, and some people were even afraid she was dying. Eventually the crying changed to laughter.

Later she was able to talk about what had taken place. She

described energy, just energy, without the sense of the personal. It was death, in a sense, because she had ceased to exist in the way she had previously known. She experienced a huge whiteness that was both utterly empty and powerful and full.

It was such a beautiful moment. She had a taste of death but was crying and moaning so strongly because she didn't want to come back. She expressed how she became expanded in this energy, out of body and mind. How could her little body contain it all? She could feel herself coming back into her body and was terrified for it. It might not be able to contain the immense energy that was her true nature.

I spoke about this to everyone that same day. I wanted to address particularly those people who were concerned for her when she had collapsed in slow motion to the floor. She was in the greatest ecstasy of her life, and they were concerned that something terrible had happened to her. She was not in her body, nor in her conditioned mind, but was somewhere else – and still awareness was present. She had a glimpse of her true nature.

A short time later I received an email question from a young French guy, who was interested in this subject of death before the death of the body.

I know a famous quotation that says simply 'to die before you die'. When I listen to Satsang I understand the message of freedom and awakening from the false self, from identifying with the body and the mind, but I don't see clearly this thing about death.

My question is: How can this death-before-death happen if we function all the time from the very place that has to die? Is it the false self that dies? And how does that happen?

I would like to change your famous quotation a bit. I would prefer to say 'to die before you die, and be reborn'. But actually that's also not really true. It is more like a metaphor for this moment of awakening. You mention the false self, or ego. It is how we identify ourselves. We've slowly, slowly acquired an identity, and we call this 'me'. It is this 'me' that's talked about in the quotation – it is this identity that should die...before the death of the body. But of course this identity is anyway false. It doesn't really exist, and if it doesn't exist it can't die.

We are very identified with our sense of self, our false self. False in the sense that it doesn't really exist even though it appears to exist. We are very attached to this appearance and the quote reminds us of a possibility – by seeing that this identification is false, we reveal the Truth. The Truth is that when all experience ceases there is nothing, and in every moment something arises from this nothing. This can be called freedom because it is free from some pre-conceived identification.

We are all going to leave the body one day, but there isn't anything that will leave. The body simply stops functioning at some point. It is just consciousness that is always present and the body is activated by this consciousness. Actually, nothing changes – bodies come, bodies go. Consciousness is like a big soup in which these bodies are appearing and disappearing. Mountains come and mountains go. Rivers come and rivers go. Consciousness is constantly in motion.

There is a continual process of death and rebirth. Whatever is happening now will be left for something new in the next moment. This is the very nature of life itself. What we could call 'death-before-death' is not referring to a physical transformation but to the transformation from identified self to freedom. The possibility of this freedom is that in knowing who we really are we can live from moment to moment in innocent spontaneity, not caring about the past and not fearing the future, and allowing and trusting life to unfold.

Be As You Are
Living Our True Nature

A short walk from the house there's a large crane by the river, which used to lift cargo in and out of boats but was then closed and turned into a great little cafe. The cabin holds a bar and a small table, with most of the tables set outside overlooking the river. Hours can go by watching the ships roll up and down the Rhine and the ducks and swans going about their business. As it's close to our house and such a sweet spot, I sometimes go there to relax or to work on something on my laptop.

I was sitting quietly at a table one morning when I saw a little girl tumble down some steps. She broke into tears then got up and rubbed her leg. Then she looked around, started singing some little song and wandered off. No one rushed to her and tried to change anything about her reaction, to tell her not to sing or not to cry or not to run down steps. Just a little moment of drama, then a song, then the next thing.

It was interesting to see that for me there is no big sign saying 'rules', just a totally authentic response at any moment. This moment is not attached to any of the old conditions; there is no dog wagging its tail or barking because it thinks that it ought to. There is no 'next thing' that only I can do and that has to be done. There is nobody doing that, there is just a huge availability. There may be the odd thought arising but it can be left far away. It doesn't have any real bite, because peace is much stronger. There is a childlike peaceful silence, delicate and subtle.

The invitation right at this moment is that you can be completely authentic. There are billions of actions that might happen in this moment and it doesn't make any difference which one occurs.

There is no judgment that this one is better or worse than the other billion; it is just an action. If it is coming with the authenticity of the moment then you can feel the Self, the Truth, the love, even the beauty – just being who you are.

Last year, a young man showed up suddenly in the community. He had been one week at university when he realised he completely didn't want what was apparently being offered to him: a good education and a bright future. He was deeply confused, not knowing why he felt great amounts of sadness and bitterness towards himself and to the world. After coming to the community he was often in tears. He came from a perfectly nice professional family background, but as a sensitive man he felt some strong division within himself that came from never really knowing who he was.

After dinner one evening, when he had again been flooded with tears and sobs, I took him aside to a quiet place where we could talk about this movement inside him, and about what he couldn't accept.

I can't allow myself to have an open heart, to love myself, to be silent, or not to be silent.

Well, the secret is that you don't have to 'allow' anything. Just be as you are. For example, this evening you are a man. Did you have to do something to be a man?

No, but what I mean is that when I'm quiet I get really silent and it's very painful. It's always like that.

It's painful to be silent?

Yes. I feel like pain happens in my heart. It's not bad pain or good pain – just pain.

What is Real? Life is About Waking Up

Is it really pain or could you also say that you feel simply touched? Maybe you contact your loving heart and you're just not so familiar with that.

Yes, it feels a bit like falling into something that's stopped.

And this stopping you're calling pain?

Yes. The crying stops and I can't go deeper. It's like a shutdown.

Who says what's deeper and who says whether the crying should stop or not? Can you just accept it as it is?

Thoughts arise and then it's so confusing and I don't know what's happening.

What you are expressing is very common. Unfortunately, in our journey of life, through our upbringing, we very often become divided. We can't accept ourselves as we are because we have come to believe we are not okay like this and we have to be different. This message comes to us in many different ways from many different sources. That's why it's so difficult just to be as we are.

Without even realising, we can't accept ourselves. We become divided because the judgments that were put on us as children are like voices that become thoughts. These thoughts stay with us. They are no longer coming from parents or society – now they are part of the structure of our minds.

We become our own judge, constantly judging ourselves that who we are is not alright. It's a funny paradox, because how can we be different? We can only be as we are.

Not wanting to be as we are is like an avoiding.

Yes. We avoid being who we are because we think it is not okay and we should be something else. So the invitation is to discover what is true here and then be that, which is happening anyway but we can't accept it.

If you could be different, you would be. If this is not the right place, you would be some other place. You are probably just discovering what it is to be free; you are discovering what it is to be yourself. And you are completely allowed, not because you are here in this community, but because you're running around on this planet.

• ——— •

Perhaps we develop the idea that we could transform into something else, something a bit better, but what could be more simple than 'be as you are'? Yet it is almost impossible because most of us are simply divided against ourselves.

We have one part, probably the part that brings us to a retreat or sits with us for a beautiful sunrise that is a kind of wi-fi system or navigation system. It's connected to a big satellite up there somewhere that we call God or existence and it's guiding us step-by-step through our lives. Sometimes we come into harmony with that and for a few moments we feel a deep sense of peace and oneness, as if everything suddenly is exactly as it should be. We call that a spiritual experience, but we are simply being who we truly are in that moment.

Unfortunately, most of the time we become identified with our other part, our story based on a character we call 'me'. This story has become very familiar over the years. It was created imperceptibly, and by identification with it we separate ourselves from our true nature. The reality of our story is that we have been conditioned against ourselves.

As you grew up you were often told it was not really acceptable to have the feelings you did. Maybe your mother told you to go outside and play at a time when actually you just wanted to be close to her. Anyway, you go outside and play, have a great time, and get totally covered in mud and grass stains. You come back in the house and perhaps she is angry that you made such a mess and couldn't you just be more careful! It may look completely normal, and it might be only a small thing, but to a sensitive child, and repeated often, it can deeply affect them. They can grow up with an apparently built-in sense of division, of always being split.

In order to be yourself you have to recognise this division and then when you feel tears, for example, you just accept them. If you feel anger, just accept the anger, if you feel unhappy, accept feeling unhappy, if you feel sad, accept feeling sad. Just allow yourself to be, with a deep acceptance, because you can't be wrong. When you accept what is, intensely and completely, it changes quite quickly to something else.

To be who you are is just given – you don't have to do anything. Not even meditate. Of course if you spend time sitting quietly that will be very supportive, but then just accept what is. Accept the thoughts, accept the feelings. The alternative is to maintain the duality of being a somebody. This takes a lot of work.

Ramana Maharshi used to say, 'Be as you are.' He didn't say, 'Be like me.' He didn't say, 'Be like that guy over there.' He said, 'Be as you are.' Actually, what can you do? Even if you spend your whole life trying to be somebody else, in the end you'll come to see that you can only be as you are. There is no other possibility. And anyway, if existence wanted you to be somebody else, then probably you would be somebody else. But probably it wanted you to just be as you are. It's a very beautiful invitation.

Most of us spend our whole lives making judgments and deciding if we like something or not. You can just imagine Death arriving, knocking on your door: 'Well, John, you've decided all the things you like and all the things you don't like. Now it's time to come with me.' Who cares? It is completely unimportant and a total waste of time.

When all our judgments drop, life is just like it is. That's it! Even if you discover all the things you like and all the things you don't like, life is still going to bring you stuff you like and stuff you dislike. It's not going to change just because you know what you prefer. And in the process, you can never be satisfied.

When we are ready to accept whatever happens and whatever we find inside, the judgments fall away and we can celebrate whatever life brings. We see paradise in ordinary life.

Seeing the possibility of real peace is a big moment. What is peace? It is accepting what is. It's very simple, actually. You're never going to change what is, so you might as well accept it. Everything is already as it should be. 'Be as you are' is pointing to the possibility that you can come into a deep inner harmony, no longer divided. You are still very much an individual but there is just being, unfolding from moment to moment, very simple.

> *A blind man walks into a store with his seeing-eye dog. All of a sudden he picks up the leash and begins swinging the dog over his head. The manager runs up to the man and asks, 'What are you doing?!!*
> *The blind man replies, 'Just looking around.'*

You are here on this planet to be empowered, to be beautiful, to be whoever you are supposed to be and to manifest this in the world. Do your dance, whatever it is. It's not so difficult. You just have to remember who you are and surrender to that, trust it.

The World
Our Mistaken Ideas

At the end of the last Easter Retreat, about thirty of us, community residents and guests, headed out along the banks of the Rhine with our arms full of picnic baskets, cushions and rugs. After only a few minutes we were directly by the water and wandering upstream to a nature reserve where the fields are grown for the wildlife and stretches of woodland border the river.

As we were walking along, a young guy who had something burning inside him slipped in beside me on the path. Seeing the natural beauty all around and being very aware of the threat the environment is under had triggered some strong feelings and ideas he had about the world that were causing him to suffer.

What really concerns me is feeling so helpless when I see things on the news about the world, like beings hurting other beings or the planet in danger, and not being able to really do anything.

Well, this is really your idea. The guy on the other side of the fence has a completely different idea and he cuts the trees down and cheats the poor. So who is right?

I don't know.

The world is full of these situations.

Yes, and I often identify strongly with these issues and feel so much internal conflict about it all.

If you saw the world as perfect the way it is, you could just relax.

Does it look perfect in your eyes, with all the conflicts and inequalities?

Yes, it's always perfect. How could it not be perfect?

Because there is so much suffering.

That's because everybody believes that they are separate. Recently in our community a woman experienced a very powerful energy phenomenon, a glimpse of her true nature. I don't see her suffering. She experiences the whole range of emotions, but her basic place in each moment is just wonder.

Has the world lost its seriousness for her?

She can't take it seriously anymore because she knows that what you are calling the world is an illusion. It's not real.

I can touch and smell and sense it. Do you really mean it doesn't exist? It is physically not there, or what do you mean?

I always avoid answering this question because if you don't know the answer already, anything I say won't be any help to you, and if you do know, then I don't need to say anything. It's an irrelevant question until you know Truth. From your limited perspective it's clearly ridiculous to say that I'm not separate from the tree, from the beauty of nature or from the suffering in the world.

Seeing all the suffering and the horrors committed against humanity and nature, it is very difficult for me to understand that the problem is within me. I get so confused and think I should be doing something, even if you say the problems are not real. It's always a big leap for me not

What is Real? Life is About Waking Up

to look out and feel pain and worry at the state of the world.

Do you really need to worry about it? On the absolute level nothing happens, so there is no need to worry. Everything is perfectly alright. On a slightly less absolute level, we live in a constantly changing dynamic universe and the cosmos wouldn't have much problem if Planet Earth didn't exist. Although we are very attached to our human life, Planet Earth wouldn't have much problem if human beings didn't exist. You could make a pretty good argument that she would be better off without us.

As I said, on the absolute level we don't need to do anything because the nature of this planet and the cosmos is that everything is working by itself. Human beings like to think that they are in control and doing everything, but this is simply not true. If we are considering things from a more relative point of view, the best thing we can do is to become more conscious.

The problem with this topic of conversation, and what I tried explaining to the young guy and have tried explaining to others before, is that if you believe yourself to be a somebody then you know the world through your senses and through an understanding based on separation: 'I am here and over there is the river, the picnic and the party guests.' If you have this kind of idea then of course the world exists, but it exists in a limited sense and it begs the question: How do we actually know things?

Up until about one hundred years ago science was absorbed in examining and understanding the world in a very limited and one-dimensional way. Newton did his experiments about gravity and apples dropping out of trees, and, whether we know it or not, this physical way of understanding the world has completely influenced our ideas.

Some time after Isaac Newton's experiments, things began to change in science. People like Niels Bohr, Rutherford and Einstein started developing theories and experiments on the nature of matter. Soon came the splitting of the atom, until then considered the smallest particle. With ever more sophisticated machines they were able to break these particles into even smaller and smaller pieces. Every time they broke the particle they discovered a little bit of something and a lot of nothing. They would give that something a name and a bit later, when they had the next machine ready, they'd break that something and again find a little bit of something and lot of nothing.

The reason I'm saying this is that it has all influenced the way we think, and the way we think influences how we perceive the world. The discoveries of these early quantum physicists were a total revolution in the understanding of matter. At the same time, many prominent scientists realised that the concept of us being separate from the world was completely false. They realised that there would have to be a new understanding that *we are all one*.

I'm not separate from the tree, from the river or the picnic. I'm not separate from you. It may sound ridiculous because with the knowledge gained from our limited senses it appears that we are all separate. If I look at that picnic basket I see a separate object, a useful cane container. But of course that's just from my very limited perception of it. The true nature of the picnic basket is that it's a little bit of something and a lot of nothing.

The world is clearly physical. You can go and climb up a tree or type on a computer. If I said they don't exist and *you* don't exist, then of course you would consider me completely screwy. But when you know who you are, then you know nothing really exists. You absolutely know that everything is one.

For those reasons I always hesitate to talk about this, but it's very interesting because what the scientists have recently discovered is exactly what the Indian, the Chinese and the Buddhist mystics have been saying for thousands of years. Matter is illusionary, not as it appears.

All our ideas about the world and 'my life' are just a fairy story that is playing in the mind. The good news is that the fairy story

What is Real? Life is About Waking Up

can be deleted from the hard drive: you press delete and it's all gone. When you wake up, in just a moment you see that 'my life' is simply a fairy story. It never really existed and in that moment its hold on you has gone. What's left is just what is.

> *Four monks were meditating in a monastery. All of a sudden the prayer flag on the roof started flapping.*
> *The younger monk came out of his meditation and said: 'Flag is flapping.'*
> *A more experienced monk said: 'Wind is flapping.'*
> *A third monk who had been there for more than twenty years said: 'Mind is flapping.'*
> *The fourth monk who was the eldest said: 'Mouths are flapping!'*

If you are a somebody who is using your senses to try and understand or appreciate the sound of the birds and the sunshine through the trees, then there is immediately separation. If you are like a video camera, just receiving the sensory information, then you become the sound of the birds, you become the sun through those trees, you become the whole ambience, the whole package of what's going on. There is no separation.

Many of us have experienced moments when suddenly it seems like everything touches us in an exceptional way. The sounds are clearer and the colours more saturated. Everything suddenly seems brighter and clearer and more vibrant. There is an amazing sense of peace inside. It's almost like time stops or becomes infinite and the whole experience is completely different from our everyday experience.

Clearly, everything in the world is always in a state of change – including the thoughts in the mind, the emotions and the body itself. However, there is something that doesn't change and that is what I like to call the eternal Self.

My advice to the young guy who walked with me along the river was to investigate what is already present and to focus on that part of him that never changes. This essential part of our nature – consciousness – is always present and absolutely untouched by issues of survival and the physical world. When you start to see the world from the space of the eternal Self, everything becomes different immediately.

Chapter 4
The Way of the Heart

*It is surrender. It is a giving up
of 'me', of 'my story'.
It is, in effect, a deconstruction or melting
away of the ego. It is a melting
away of the one that knows,
the one that judges,
the one that does something.
Surrender, or devotion, means a deep giving up,
an offering to God.
God is everywhere and God is everything; God is also you.
It is surrender to each moment's unfolding.*

Chapter 4
The Way of the Heart

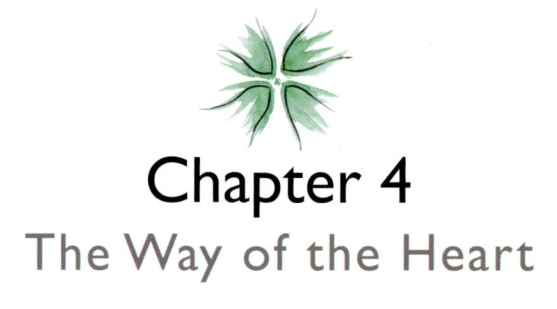

In the West we are very reliant on the mind and emotions to guide us through life. The Way of the Heart is about connecting to our inner navigation system, our intuition, and trusting in the flow of life. It is about living with an open heart, which means trust and surrender to what life brings. When you can trust in life as it is, from the heart, you experience an expansiveness and openness beyond emotions and the thinking mind.

Way of the Heart 101
Devotion, Trust and Surrender

Hopeless in the Desert 108
Letting Go and Being Present

The Navigation System 114
Guidance From the Heart

Way of Beauty 120
Rediscovering Our Senses

Conscious Parenting 127
Raising Children With Awareness

Way of the Heart
Devotion, Trust and Surrender

Every year I'm drawn to Tiruvannamalai, a small town in South India. One of my spiritual heroes, Sri Ramana Maharshi, lived there his whole life, guiding the development of an ashram around him at the foot of the holy mountain, Arunachala. So it is here that I find myself at the start of the year. I am staying in an ashram overlooking the mountain with a group of thirty-five students in a residential retreat for three weeks.

Something about the energy and pace of India, especially in this little town, really confronts anyone who has been living too long in their own private western ways, living in a well-furbished apartment in a well-organised city. They have their circle of friends, their social security, their family close by and their comfortable job. For a person coming from this situation, the general chaos and disorderly vibrancy of India is sure to be a great shake-up.

Mila had come to Satsang in Germany and had followed her interest in Truth and come to India, after much doubt. She lived a comfortable life and had never really looked at herself in the kind of honest way that Satsang encourages.

During the Indian retreat we always make a three or four day bus trip to visit various Indian masters. Thirty-five people piled into one Indian bus for four days, sharing everything, makes for an intense experience, which, as it turned out, Mila was very resistant to try. She outright refused in the beginning, but was able to see that she was resistant because of certain conditionings or rooted ideas she had in her mind. Early on the day before the bus trip she found me on the balcony of the ashram.

The thing I need this moment is some help to get onto the bus. Yesterday, after speaking with Cheryl and Meera who offered to be my support team, I decided to go on the trip. The promise of their support helped me to say yes – but I am shivering with fear! I am trying to surrender, telling myself, 'Get in! You can trust everyone. You can trust existence!' But it's not working. So I need some help to get onto the bus.

I know a little story. You won't like it so much, but maybe you'll remember it.

There's a lady sitting on a bus. As she sits on this bus, the other passengers notice that she's getting very nervous. Finally one of the passengers asks her, 'Are you okay?' And she says, 'Well, actually, I'm getting quite nervous that I might miss my stop.' So they ask her, 'Well, which is your stop?' She replies, 'My stop is the bus depot.'

We are all like this, you see. We're on the bus and it is going to take us to the bus depot. Maybe we all have a different destination, but we're all on the bus and we don't really have to worry about it because it's all taken care of. You may not remember, but you didn't really decide to come on the bus – to be born into this world. You just arrived.

And when you leave, you leave. You don't really decide that either. These are probably the two most important events of your life, and they just happen – no decision needed. And things like, 'What proportion of oxygen in the air do I need?' you probably don't decide that either. Every day it all just happens. When you can begin to understand this you can surrender, you can relax. So it's nice that two kind human beings named Cheryl and Meera will take care of you, but actually the job's already being done. Do you see this?

I don't quite understand.

Everybody and everything is already taking care of you. Your mind would like to have two special carers, but you're already being cared for.

Way of the Heart

Intellectually I know this, but I can't feel it and my fears overcome this knowing.

Well, this is very honest. Already you can see that in the first ten days of this retreat you have been cared for. From the trust that came out of this caring you made the decision to come with us on the bus trip. So it's already happening. Something is opening and a deep understanding of trust is already surfacing. This is your issue. As life unfolds we receive many knocks that make it difficult to trust.

Yes. This may jolly well be a chance to get over these fears and more into the trust.

Yes, and not only for you. You are a dramatic example, but actually, in quieter or less obvious ways it is the same for everybody. Not everyone can trust. In fact, hardly anyone can trust completely.

You are able to trust enough to take a step towards your fear of the unknown. You think something awful will happen to you on the bus trip, and you believe that with every fibre of your being.

Traditionally, there are two paths to Self-realisation. There's the Way of Knowledge and the Way of the Heart. Very different, but they come to the same Truth. The Way of Knowledge leads to a moment of understanding where you realise that the construction 'my life', which you have been building for many years, doesn't exist, that it was always an illusion.

The Way of the Heart – devotion – leads to Truth through surrender. You constantly surrender to existence everything that you know to be 'me'. You constantly give up everything into the fire. In this way you come to the same Truth. Because of the many small surrenders, this big 'me', the illusion, is simply given up into the fire, and in that moment it ceases to exist. Either way, the ego, the false self, will be seen not to exist. Either way, it's a total death of the 'I'.

The Way of the Heart

As soon as you get off the plane in India the air is dripping with devotion. When you pass through little villages or towns, or when you walk anywhere in India, you can immediately feel devotion. It's hanging in the air. Everywhere you go there are little glimpses: temples, small shrines, offerings, maybe a garland around a cow's neck. Little signs of devotion are everywhere.

But devotion is really not on the outside. It's not about the shrine or the garland. It's actually about what happens inside you. This is an important part of all my work – to watch the heart opening and see how it can be expressed though giving. When we're making prayers, what the Indians call puja, or making an offering of flowers or incense to one of the gods, something happens inside us. It's rather similar to what happens in the West when we pray in a sincere way.

It is surrender. It is a giving up of 'me'. It is, in effect, a deconstruction or melting away of the ego. It is a melting away of the one that knows, the one that judges, the one that does something. Surrender, or devotion, means a deep giving up, an offering to God. God is everywhere and God is everything; God is also you. It is surrender to each moment's unfolding.

It is about giving up the knower and giving up everything inside you that you think you know. It can be a little scary. You can become terrified. Surrender can only work if there is deep trust. In the West we have difficulty trusting anything or anyone. We only trust our 'story' – which is a pity, really. The Way of the Heart is about opening. When you are living in that openness you can feel how easy it is to trust and surrender. When you meet someone who has a very open heart, or is very much in their heart, then you'll have a sense of this person being with themselves and pulsating with energy. There is a lot of joy, fun, spontaneity and playfulness. When you have a deep trust your whole being opens to life. You become available.

We can get a sense of this when we sing traditional Indian mantras. They have a particular energy and have been specifically created to open the energy systems of the body. When you sing these mantras you can really feel an opening, and if you put your whole energy into them something really tremendous happens. Singing the same mantra on and on, for hours and hours, without any point, you simply disappear. You're gone. There's nobody home. This is a wonderful moment of divine drunkenness. Surrender could happen.

By surrender I'm talking about accepting the moment as it is, saying yes to the moment. By not surrendering you are actually saying yes to the false self. You are saying yes to 'me'. 'I' am deciding not to accept what is happening. Who is this 'I' that's deciding? Well, of course, it is the false self. It is the part of the mind that has ideas. We do this all the time without realising what we are really choosing. When you are not accepting the moment, as it is, then what you are really doing is giving power to the false self.

Careful awareness is needed because there is always the possibility of being caught up with the 'I'. When we are caught up we pull ourselves back into the false self. You can't really decide to surrender but you can live a surrendered life. You can live with an open yes, and when you have this open yes there is acceptance.

Along with surrender, trust is needed. They go together. As you trust more, the surrender can go deeper, and the deeper you surrender the easier it is to trust.

You can't really experience love unless you can open your heart and trust. We have all had moments of being open hearted and then closing down because of some pain. So we have some history around love, around an open heart. We are not so trusting about it. Love is about trust.

> *A climber fell off a cliff, and as he tumbled down he caught hold of a small branch and just managed to hang on.*
> *'Help! Is there anybody up there?' he shouted.*
> *A majestic voice boomed through the gorge: 'I will help you, my son, but first you must have faith in me.'*
> *'Yes, yes, I trust you!' cried the man.*
> *'Let go of the branch,' boomed the voice.*
> *There was a long pause, and the man shouted up again, 'Is there anyone else up there I could talk to?'*

The Way of the Heart

Fundamental to trust is an acceptance of what is, even when you think, for whatever reason, whatever judgment, for whatever idea, that you don't like it. This already sounds very uncomfortable and challenging, but it has an enormous effect. If you continually surrender your personal wanting you find that all your judgments, ideas, desires and comparisons start to disappear and you feel closer to the Self, closer to existence, closer to your own essence. It just happens. While you are busy 'being right' in your personal 'I', you are keeping yourself away; you are creating separation.

Service is a beautiful way to open the heart, let go of personal wanting and disappear into the Self. For example, just giving for no reason and with no expectation of a return. In ashrams and monasteries the attendants and monks are all in service. What are they in service to? Who are they in service to? We could say to existence and the divine work.

Washing dishes in the kitchen obviously doesn't bring you anything. Maybe you get a little tired, but if you keep washing the dishes you find that in the end something happens. In this simple service, the whole energy system can open up. The heart opens and the ego, this separate me, starts to dissolve and deconstruct.

True service comes from the heart, along with compassion and humility. When you do service in a heartfelt way, then you get the benefit of an open heart.

Watch what happens in your life, and, wherever appropriate, find ways to serve others. Giving will open your heart and allow the trust to come.

I would like to share a personal story of trust. Every full moon in Tiruvannamalai, hundreds of thousands of people walk around the holy mountain, Arunachala, following a particular path and paying homage at countless small and large shrines along the way. It is a river of humanity.

Flowing along with half a million people I had a very special experience. I had become separated from the people I was walking with at one of the busiest spots on the walk, the heart of the main temple of the town. It was extremely crowded and in the middle of this great press of bodies were two wizened, beautiful old sadhus dressed in their traditional orange robes and sitting on the ground. One had his eyes closed and the other was chanting a mantra with just some bells to accompany him. I felt to offer them something. I decided to buy some orange blankets, which were being sold at a nearby stall. I found I had far too little money and couldn't buy what I wanted.

Then all of a sudden, out of the huge crowd, a friend who I hadn't seen for some months appeared. When he saw me he came over and gave me some money he owed me. Existence had arranged that just as I needed some money this friend appeared. How is that possible?

We put so much energy into planning and controlling so that we can always have what we believe we want. But we forget. We don't trust and so don't allow this bigger possibility to do it for us. I have so many stories like this happening on a daily basis.

Trust is something that we are not so good at. We are good at trusting our own mind, but this is not the trust I am talking about. I'm talking about trusting what is, even when it doesn't fit with our ideas. Life is simply unfolding. Can we just accept it?

Hopeless in the Desert
Letting Go and Being Present

If ever there was a time when I could say I was hopeless in the desert, it was just after a particularly beautiful time in my life. It is very mysterious how the events fitted together and how the synchronicity played out perfectly. I got to see clearly that even in times that are incredibly hard or full of suffering, everything always works out.

I had been living in India for about seven years, five of them with my spiritual master, Papaji. Finally it was time to go. In order to stay in India for such a long time, I had to get some slightly illegal help with my visa. It was not one hundred percent legitimate, but rather an acceptable practice in India at that time.

Without thinking anything about it, because for many years I hadn't been thinking so much, I got on a plane in Delhi to fly to Australia. I would just say here that after having been with a spiritual master for five years I felt very good, but I hadn't really been tested.

Some friends were waiting for me in Australia with a dinner party organised. But unfortunately, existence had other ideas. I arrived in Bangkok at eight o'clock in the morning to find my flight delayed. I was offered a hotel for the duration of my time at the airport. Immediately my mind got very excited at the prospect as it imagined the comfortable room and lovely meal, so different from India. I handed over my passport to the immigration officials and before I knew what was happening some armed guards came up to me, put me in handcuffs and marched me away. I was obviously a bit shocked and was asking what was going on as they pulled me away. I was arrested and I spent three weeks in a Thai jail. Needless to say, my dinner in Australia got cold!

Once released on bail I spent two months getting out of

Thailand. It was a tough time. I had never been in prison and I guess Thai prisons are among the least desirable. I was the only westerner in my block, so naturally I got to sleep next to the toilet with fifty hardened criminals around me. But the interesting thing was I felt absolutely free. I wouldn't say I was particularly happy, but there was an inner ground where I felt completely free.

One of the memorable moments of this experience was when I had to go to the court from prison. I had to wake particularly early that morning and wear a nice little brown outfit – short brown pants and a brown button-up shirt. Then they put leg irons around my ankles, with a chain between, which I had to lift with a string in order to walk. I got on a bus with maybe fifty other prisoners, all in leg irons, and we were taken to court where we had to wait in a big cage, all clanking our chains.

It was interesting that someone always showed up to support and help me. In each of three different blocks someone always fed me. In the first block I was fed on delicious home cooking. Once I was out on bail the British Embassy gave amazing support, a new passport and the advice to flee Thailand as I would never get a fair trial. I discovered escaping from a country was harder than getting out of prison. Existence took care of me, and one day out at the beach I bumped into a real criminal who was kind enough to arrange my departure!

All this didn't really fit with my idea of a nice Thai hotel, but it was, in fact, very interesting. Looking back, many things happened in that time, including the threat of being killed. It was a tough lesson, but even in prison I discovered I was really free. Nothing affected it. It is possible to accept everything if there is a deep trust in life.

Although my physical freedom was curtailed and the accommodation was hardly five star, I felt an inner peace that nothing could effect. Later I could see the value of my prison experience coming the day after leaving my master. It was clear that there was a peace and power that nothing on the outside could touch.

We always want to change the situation we are in or the feelings we have. Recently I went to Berlin to give Satsang and I spoke with

The Way of the Heart

a man who could not accept the results of his meditation. He had ideas about how it should be and was blind to what was actually happening for him.

I keep having the experience that when it is still both inside and outside there is nothing to do and there is nobody I can somehow relate to. Then a big emptiness, like a wilderness or desert comes and I can't manage to meet that and go through it.

When you come to this desert space, does it feel welcoming or not so welcoming?

It's not comfortable, not nice. It's just very boring. My longing is to be happy with myself, intoxicated with myself.

It sounds like you have some strong ideas about it. It's boring and you want it to be intoxicating. What if I told you that this desert is yourself? Could you just completely accept the boredom?

I tried that, but then I thought, 'Oh no! I can't manage that.' The other day a friend said to me, 'Why do you go to Satsang when you are such a hopeless case?' It was really a big joy for me to hear that. I was totally fascinated. I was overjoyed, relieved, but I don't know why. It doesn't sound so positive, actually.

Being absolutely hopeless is very positive, and in fact I often say you are only ready for Satsang when you have given up all hope. When you try to manage everything you are activating the mind, and when you just accept everything as it is, it's boring. I remember once being bored for about three months. It wasn't so easy to accept, but it got much worse if I didn't. By not accepting life as it is, what you are really saying is, 'I don't like it like this. I would like it like that. Here is boring desert and over there is piles of joy, which is what I would really like.' This is the source of all our trouble, and peace, which is quite a good word for happiness, arrives immediately we accept life as it is, without any desire to change it.

The invitation is just to be here now, accepting hopelessness, boredom, or whatever it is. Of course, this is not so easy because we have been very conditioned to try to get what we want. We have many ideas of how it should be – no boredom, let's have joy! Amazingly, as soon as you accept the boredom then it opens and changes and moves to joy. From joy it goes to peace and then beyond peace to love, which is our true nature.

I can see how my mind starts up and says, 'Aha! Now I have to tolerate this loneliness and emptiness so that in the end maybe love comes.'

When you use the word 'tolerate' it suggests there is something better. But we are talking about your true nature. That is the best.

And are you saying that for me at the moment the desert is the best, and nothing else?

If that's what's happening, that's what's happening. My guess is that you have some ideas and judgments about this desert but somebody else might call it emptiness, no-mind. Maybe you are not as hopeless as your friends think you are!

Normally we are very involved in 'doing'. Being in the desert where nothing much is happening is a good place from which to question who it is that is 'doing' so much. You can focus on the question, 'Who am I?'

My thinking, my mind, tries to answer it and it conjures up many pictures.

Yes, yes, minds do that. But with this question you are looking for a much deeper answer and, in fact, you are looking for an answer a bit like your desert – boring. We have been strongly conditioned with the idea that we must be very active, experiencing excitement and piles of joy and love, like Action Man. But if you drop your idea about Action Man and accept the boring old desert, then you will probably find that all your days in Satsang have been rewarded. Being hopeless is beautiful, because then you can see what is incredibly close and incredibly simple.

Any hope you have keeps you from the emptiness because it keeps you in a perpetual cycle of desire where you hope that you could just get … something, anything. 'If I could just go to India, that would be it! If I could just meet a great saint!' Or perhaps all you want is an ice cream. Maybe you would like a new lover. Lovers are always good – you can project a lot onto them. 'If I can just find the right lover then I will be alright.' Big hope, and for some time, of course, we feel rather good with that.

We have all experienced New Year's Eve, the thirty-first of December. As midnight strikes, hope reaches a peak because this year was really awful but next year is going to be really great! Unfortunately, by about three o'clock the next afternoon it's rather similar to last year, and so all your hope comes crashing down. So actually, hopeless is really good. If you have a lot of hope you are always looking to the future. This week is terrible, but next week is going to be great!

I was in Sydney when it was not just a new year but something much greater – it was the New Millennium. Wow! It seemed that it was to be something really special as it only happens every thousand years. There was so much hope. They had been planning months ahead how to make the New Millennium really special. This is how the human mind works. You only feel good when there is hope that the future will be wonderful, even if now in the present you suffer.

If you really want to change this suffering then you need to see the illusion of hope that you hold inside your own mind. It is the only thing that prevents you living in a divine way. When you come to this emptiness – an absence of you – then suddenly you are aware

Hopeless in the Desert

of the breeze on your body, the birds, the hooting of the traffic, the presence of nature. Everything moves in very easy ways. You realise that right now you feel very, very good, without doing anything.

As you relax into your own nature, you discover at the same time a feeling of wellbeing. I really want to encourage you to stay with yourself. Then you'll discover you don't need anything to make you feel good – because you are already good. This is where you will find what you're looking for.

> *Sherlock Holmes and Dr Watson go on a camping trip, set up their tent, and fall asleep. Some hours later, Holmes wakes his faithful friend.*
> *'Watson, look up at the sky and tell me what you see.'*
> *Watson replies, 'I see millions of stars.'*
> *'What does that tell you?'*
> *Watson ponders for a minute. 'Astronomically speaking, it tells me that there are millions of galaxies and potentially billions of planets. Astrologically, it tells me that Saturn is in Leo. Time wise, it appears to be approximately a quarter past three. Theologically, it's evident the Lord is all-powerful and we are small and insignificant. Meteorologically, it seems we will have a beautiful day tomorrow. What does it tell you?'*
> *Sherlock Holmes is silent for a moment, then says, 'Someone has stolen our tent.'*

If you have any hope at all it puts you back into the game of 'my life'. You will start looking out into the world and saying to yourself, 'If I could just climb up to the top of that mountain there would be so much good energy that "poof!" – that will do it!' When you live in hope you are living for the future. This is a device that the mind uses to escape from now. Living in hopelessness you are living absolutely in the moment.

The Navigation System
Let Your Heart Guide You

It was a spring weekend in the elegant city of Paris where I had come to hold Satsang and connect to the French culture. On the Saturday, I was invited to a friend's house for dinner and discovered a wonderful tea, called something like Empress Tea. As I am English I love a good tea and I was interested to buy it. I got the directions to the shop where it could be found, but my friend warned me that it was in a maze of little streets and squares, very hard to find. There was only a little time between dinner and my evening meeting so I gave up my hopes of the teashop for that evening.

The next day I found myself with some friends walking around an old area of the city, with many winding streets and beautiful buildings. I could feel it happening very strongly that, as usual, I was not paying attention to directions and maps but just following some kind of unspoken internal navigation system. The people I was with began to get a bit exasperated by all the twists and turns that I was making, especially when I would just disappear from behind them and head off down a dark side alley.

After walking like this for some time we suddenly popped out onto a little street and came face to face with the very teashop I had been told about the day before. We had wandered without a plan and without ideas and had arrived at exactly the place we wanted to be.

I must say that I never worry about whether or not I will find a place I am looking for. There is a feeling of knowing, even if I don't actually know anything in the sense of a certain fixed knowledge. Countless times in my life I have been in new places and I always find myself easily navigated to shops, restaurants, art galleries and other places that I resonate with. If I am with students or friends

The Navigation System

they are always surprised by how randomly I seem to wander around and how mysteriously we arrive at places that suit us perfectly. All the big decisions in my life have happened in this way, even finding my spiritual masters.

In the meeting that evening I described what had happened and talked about the internal navigation system. It was this that had led us slowly through the twisting streets of Paris to the wonderful teashop and then to get the right bus back just in time for Satsang. After I had introduced the topic, a French man came to sit with me. Before he began talking, I asked him how he had decided to come to this meeting.

•———•

I would say the navigation system caught me, and I didn't resist.

Right. What I'm calling the navigation system is always there; it's always operating, always taking you – guiding your whole life, actually. You only have to say yes. The judgments we make about whether something is good or not are not important at all. Better to trust the navigation system.

You can always feel when there's a yes because everything opens and flows. When you hold onto some strong ideas or structures in the mind then the flow can't happen.

I tried hanging on for a long time, but it doesn't work!

You get a headache.

Yes. This little difference, I know it very well. I sit with an issue, thinking I can't come out of it. Then I try saying yes, yes, yes, but it doesn't change. The only thing that helps is not taking it seriously: 'Okay, the heart is closed. Good.' And then something relaxes and it can open. It happened! Now I feel that even if I wanted to I couldn't close my heart. I can't change what is, and also I can't say, 'Wow! I opened my heart.'

Yes, these things just happen, and a strong cloud of mind also just happens.

But the biggest hindrance in my case was how to get out of the mind with the mind.

But you're not still trying to do that.

Not so much anymore.

It's a common misunderstanding in spiritual circles that we have to stop the mind. This means struggling with thoughts and we end up with a headache!

Can I assume that this state of opening will close again? Maybe this opening and closing is like day and night or summer and winter.

I don't think it has to be like that. It's possible to live with an open heart. For that there needs to be a big yes, without any idea that this would be better, that would be better, I'd like it like that, I don't like it like this. These preferences have to fall away, and if you have a strong sense of yes then you can stay with an open heart.

Do you think it can grow and grow until it becomes a permanent state?

I don't know about growing and growing, but you can permanently be open, yes. In a way, you could say it's more natural to live with your energy system simply open.

•———•

We're looking to have a quieter mind and to increase our awareness. This allows us to penetrate to something we can say is our very nature, our essence, our being, the Self. The navigation system is a metaphor for this beingness, this essence. Living with a direct connection, it brings us more trust and more surrender to life itself. In a way, our navigation system works exactly like a car's. What's connected to our hearts is not a satellite, of course, but rather the whole energy of existence. Living in this direct connection to our being we get the messages that are meant for us. It brings us constant guidance as our lives unfolds. It is always guiding us but usually we are so caught up in our thoughts and feeling that we don't recognise it. Living in openness we feel how easy it is to trust and surrender.

Although we might have the idea of being a nicely sealed little package, separate from everything else, the reality is we are an absolutely integrated part of the whole. We are guided through life by all kinds of energetic phenomena, which are acting on the earth and on us whether we are aware of it or not.

I have no idea how it all works, but I do know that when I'm not so busy with thoughts and I become quiet, it's as if I'm being directed. There is an instantaneous 'knowing'.

There have been times in my life when I would get a bit nervous about simple daily decisions, such as 'Will I go in the afternoon or the morning?' Sometimes I would even write a list of pros and cons, feeling I had to get the right answer.

Nowadays it's not like that. If I'm quiet then there is nearly always a clear 'knowing', and even if it's not clear I just choose one and go with that – because it doesn't really matter. I know on a deeper level that it doesn't actually matter where I end up. If I go in the morning, I'll end up with lunch. If I go in the afternoon, I'll end up with dinner.

There are other times when, for whatever reason, things are not so relaxed, not so quiet, and perhaps I can feel something a bit contracted. There are a lot of thoughts and I don't really have any sense of knowing. I get a little tense and try to work it out. But even in this situation, when I am not aware of this 'knowing', the navigation system is still operating.

For example, I thought I was going to be an architect. I worked it all out – I studied and got my piece of paper saying 'now you're an architect', but somehow it didn't happen, or only for a short

The Way of the Heart

while. At that time I was not interested in India or Indian gurus but unexpected things happened and I ended up in India visiting an India guru. Out of that situation my whole life went in a very different direction. How did that happen? I don't really know, but I can only assume it happened because of this navigation system. It was guiding me in a direction I wasn't familiar with.

Apparently, when the founder of Apple, Steve Jobs, was interviewed about the iPad, he was asked what kind of consumer research they had done for the new product. He said they hadn't done any. How could people give any opinion when they didn't know the incredible possibility of the iPad? Similarly, Henry Ford did no consumer research before introducing the first motorcars into the market. Presumably, the people of the time would have suggested a faster horse. What could I have decided about India and an Indian guru if I had no knowledge about it and the incredible doorways it could open in my life?

So, after many years of struggling with the thoughts in my mind, nowadays I simply accept this deeper knowing. I am not concerned about making wrong decisions because everything is just the game of life playing out, and I can enjoy the game.

> *A young man is driving his new sports car along a quiet country lane. There's no traffic about so he risks accelerating to ninety kilometres per hour, then one hundred and then one hundred and ten. He rounds a bend and all of a sudden sees two old farmers standing in the middle of the road chatting. The man pulls the steering wheel sharply to one side, the car shoots up an embankment, flies into the air, and crashes in the middle of an adjacent field.*
>
> *Observing this, one of the farmers turns to the other and says, 'That was lucky, Fred. I think we got out of that field just in time.*

Eventually we will come to a moment of conscious understanding. Instead of being locked into the false self we come one day to an

The Navigation System

understanding where we realise that we are the Self. In that moment the attachment to this individual bubble travelling separately through the universe is completely dissolved and you realise that you are absolutely part of everything. There's an enormous relaxation, and that's it. From then on you will be consciously aware that you are being guided by this navigation system.

It is common that people are suddenly, for no obvious reason, thrown into a great openness where there is tremendous peace, stillness, love and wellbeing. This is our true nature, a constant that is always there. If we are quiet enough, if we are able to detach from the busyness of the mind, then there's a possibility that we can consciously realise the navigation system. People often describe wonderful and powerful synchronicity in their lives where something happened and it felt completely right. This is the navigation system.

Life becomes very relaxed, because whenever something needs to happen you will be consciously moved by your navigation system. I'm talking about trusting life, trusting what is, surrendering to the flow of your life – not fighting against what is.

Way of Beauty
Rediscovering Our Senses

Walking through the garden we have at the back of the house, I met Elena, the resident in charge of the gardens and the zoo. She has been living in the community for about four years now, and through many years of meditation and self-awareness she understands a lot about herself and has had many openings into her true nature. She also has a quality of innocence about her. However, she still has a strong tendency to be very involved in her stories and her mind and to chatter endlessly about them. She seems to be stuck in this, not knowing a way to come out of it. As expected, she started telling me her stories, how she was stuck and how she had this and that running in her mind and body.

We were standing in the middle of the beautiful garden, with trees flowering all around us, raspberries fresh on the bushes, and butterflies and insects busy amongst the flowers. Elena couldn't be there for that beauty because of all the old stories in her mind. There was this paradise around us and yet it was being missed by the very person who was developing and nurturing it, and who could actually gain the most benefit from just being there, letting the beauty sink in.

I stopped her so that I could immediately address this absorption that held her in her stories.

Elena, we often talk about peace, love and emptiness, but right now I would like to talk about beauty. For the next step in your life, in this abundance of spring, I suggest you practise while you're gardening – it's the perfect place to let all these old stories disappear.

The invitation is just to be here.

I have never really thought about the garden like that.

Traditionally, there are two paths to awakening. There's the Way of Knowledge, through the intellect, and there's the Way of the Heart, which is deep surrender. However, there's also the Way of Beauty, and you're in exactly the right place for that. You can just drown in the beauty because everything that you're working with in the garden is from existence; it is all God. You're touching God all day. The garden is a very beautiful laboratory.

Yes, I have noticed that over some time the garden has drawn me in, especially since we have bought all the new plants.

Be aware that even if you are not speaking out your stories they are still running in your mind. When you come into the garden, look around and find a place that really attracts you, a little corner somewhere that draws you to it. Then, at the beginning and end of your work, just sit there for five or ten minutes. Choose a different spot each day. You'll find that after a week or two of this conscious recognition of beauty there will be something different in your life because all those five-minute sittings will come together inside you. Just fall into the beauty.'

Thank you, I'll try it.

This peace can also manifest in relation to a beautiful art work. Art can come from the artist's mind, or it can come from the Self, from presence, from deep inside. This form of art is an expression of the Way of Beauty.

The other day some friends and I went to an art fair in Holland. It has been running for twenty-five years and has a policy that everything has to be a very high standard. There is modern art, furniture, classical pieces, antiques, European, Asian and works from all over the world. When we went in, I was immediately aware of the quality; one stall had three Picassos.

We walked around for six hours, and it felt like being in Satsang. There was so much beauty in that place. It didn't really matter whether we liked the art works or not, but the effect of just walking around in that fair all day was such a feeling of peace. It was like being transported to paradise, where everywhere you look there is beauty. Everyone seemed very open – surely an effect of the incredible beauty. The whole day was amazing, 'Wow!'

A man at the fair told me that during the Second World War, members of the British government wanted to cut off funding for the arts as it was deemed non-essential for the war effort. It is reputed that Winston Churchill said to these people, 'What are we fighting this war for?' This really makes you think about beauty and the importance of the creative arts. It is almost the highest expression of our existence as human beings.

There is a reason why certain art works appeal to almost everyone. Their beauty touches something inside, and it has to do with the artist being a channel while creating it. I was walking in the Grand Gallery in The Louvre where there are many, many paintings one above the other. As I walked through I was aware of the beauty and brilliance of the paintings, but then I found myself stopping in front of one particular painting because something about it had touched me more than the others.

I looked at the label and saw it was a famous painting by Leonardo da Vinci. Standing there I realised that its beauty is a kind of transmission from the artist. The artist was probably a very free individual, so there is a certain peace coming through his work. The Mona Lisa is famous for that – in her smile is peace. This peace is the peace of Leonardo da Vinci, and it is transmitted to us.

Just standing there I was communicating with the artist in the same way we sit together in Satsang. It's not about the words. It's not about your character, your personality – nothing like that. It's something about the inner sense of silence and the peace.

It's the artist's peace, my peace, but also our peace. And what is peace? What does it mean? It is a deep contentment; a feeling that it's okay here and there's no need to change anything. No desire – this is peace. Just to be here, now. All good classical art has become great because, in its own way, it brings us to that inner harmony.

Michelangelo was twenty-one when he carved the famous Pieta in the Vatican from a single piece of marble. Even though well trained in sculpting, how is it possible that someone can create such incredible beauty, especially at such a young age? Are skill, knowledge and depth of perception enough? I would suggest that the power of consciousness uses someone who is particularly receptive and skilled, like Michelangelo, as the hand to make the sculpture. It's not personal. We like to say, 'Oh, Michelangelo made that,' but it comes from that still place of beauty inside, which will certainly have a unique flavour in every human being, but can never be called 'personal'.

> 'Oh Doctor, Doctor!' said the woman, running into the room, 'I simply have to tell you all the things that are wrong with me!'
> The man surveyed her from head to foot. 'Madam, I've three things to tell you. First, your weight needs reducing by nearly ten kilograms. Second, your beauty would be improved if you use about one-tenth as much make-up and lipstick. And third, I am an artist; you will find the doctor next door.'

What I'm suggesting is that if the artist is painting or sculpting out of his very Self, then this communicates through the art and it has the power to take you there also. If art is made out of some idea, if it is made largely from the mind, then you might like it, you might find it interesting, but I doubt it has this power.

When you're attracted to art, to architecture, to classical music, to the beauty of nature, to anything that you call beautiful, it is a trigger for something happening inside you. You can understand life as a play or an expression of the inner emptiness. When you become really quiet and nothing is moving, then there is no impetus to go anywhere, nothing to do, and suddenly something wants to express – this is creativity. This movement of creativity creates the form, which, in turn, touches us as beautiful.

I went with a friend to the centre of Kiev, in Ukraine, where I hold retreats every year. He suggested we go to a modern art exhibition in a gallery nearby.

The artist was Anish Kapoor, an Indian-English sculptor. I had come across his work about thirty years ago in a small art gallery in London. Anyway, as we went up through the building, through the small galleries, I realised the incredible quality of the works. They were way beyond liking and disliking and touched some deep part of me.

Higher up there were some paintings and sculptures from other very well known international artists and at the top of the building was an amazing cafe. The food, the presentation, the tastes were out of this world. I ordered a fish salad, which came with a small muslin bag tied with a little string. The little bag was so simple and so beautiful. Inside was a segment of lemon and when I realised the purpose of the bag I immediately fell in love with the restaurant. You know how it is with lemons? You squeeze them and the pips come out all over your food. Not in this restaurant, thanks to the little muslin bag!

I am not using the word beauty as the opposite of ugly, but rather to suggest the ultimate rightness of harmony and proportion in creation itself. We experience this inside when we are deeply touched by something on the outside – a flower, an artwork, a particular building, a beautiful sunset or innocent children. We become aware that we are in fact part of creation. Harmony and proportion are creation itself. We feel a deep connectedness and then we experience beauty. Any judgment about beauty or ugliness is simply irrelevant. It's more to do with a universal proportion, a universal harmony.

The beauty is you, *your* beauty. You feel inspired, and you come inside to what is true. If you live like that you will almost certainly attract beautiful things to you. It just happens. But it's not really about beauty. It's about that place inside you, and when you make *that* the priority of your life, then you are led to your essence. We have the possibility to live out of that place – not just from the rather shallow part of the mind but from 'deep inside'.

Interestingly, it's not really spiritual. Maybe we need a word and so we use 'spiritual', but it does tend to separate us from the ordinary life. It's about life itself, actually. You can live your life asleep, as a kind of sophisticated robot, or you can demand freedom from your own cage, your own prison. You have created your prison and don't even realise it. When you do, you're just as likely to continue in the prison because it feels too dangerous to go outside.

It's not dangerous. It's a benevolent universe that wants to give us only good stuff. It's all good, even when it's not being good. For example, I had to get off of a train recently at five o'clock in the morning. I only really see the sunrise when I travel overnight because usually I'm never up that early. I had a severe pain in my back and I hadn't slept much during the night. I could barely walk, and the pain was so intense it felt like hot knives were sliding across my spine. Then suddenly I saw these chimneys on the skyline sending out piles of smoke. The smoke was connecting to the dark clouds and swirling above the quiet world below. It was a beautiful sunrise, even though it wasn't easy on the eye and I was in terrible pain.

Without doubt, if you are in a harmonious and peaceful inner state then many things appear to be beautiful. When you are not in that state, then a lot of things feel wrong or chaotic or in some way out of harmony. How we experience the world, in fact, depends upon our inner state.

Watch your own life. When you're quiet, watch what comes out of that. You may well find yourself drawn to dance, music, painting or some other form of creative expression. When you come to your own inner beauty and peace, when the neurotic mind stops, then consciousness wants to express itself. Even ordinary things like sweeping the floor or digging the garden can be outlets for creativity.

In reality, everything is an expression of consciousness. I remember a Satsang in a beautiful park in India with my spiritual teacher, Papaji. We were all gathered round and as he walked towards us I couldn't help looking at him and, as always, I was moved by the sight of him. But then suddenly, between where I was sitting and where Papaji was walking, I noticed a big pile of cow dung. Just for a moment my attention went from Papaji to the cow dung. Papaji was obviously beautiful, but what about the cow dung. Was it also beautiful? I realised in that moment that I couldn't make any distinction.

I remembered this, years later, when a baby who had been born in the community was learning to speak. The first words to come out of his little mouth weren't 'mummy' or 'daddy', 'cat' or 'dog', they were 'kaka' (shit) and 'Buddha'.

If you are receptive and if there is enough emptiness inside, then everything appears beautiful. Beauty is never ending and is the same as Truth. It comes from the same place inside.

Conscious Parenting
Raising Children with Awareness

To cross the wide river that lies almost directly outside my front door, you have to take a small ferry that ships people, bikes and cars from early morning till evening. There's a lovely feeling of crossing over, and I often take a break to go across to the other side where there is a nature reserve for long walks and a great cafe that overlooks the river.

One afternoon recently I was sitting in this cafe with a friend. There was a couple there with a little boy. He looked very well cared for and I guess he was about five years old. We both noticed him because he was very happy, active, and inquisitive.

There was a moment when the boy ran off from the table and started to explore the coffee shop a bit. Immediately the mother got up and brought him back to their table. She didn't do it in a bad way, and when she got him back to the table she sat him on her knee, bounced him up and down, and it was all rather sweet.

I had such a strong feeling of what the little boy would have liked to tell his mother, and for that matter what many other children would like to say:

'Just leave me alone for a bit. I'd like to explore the cafe. Maybe I'd like to go and talk to those nice people over there. Love me, but give me space. I don't belong to you. Be touched that I'm in your hands for some time. I'm not your possession. I understand there has to be some discipline. I understand there have to be some boundaries. I understand that you have to take care I don't run across the road and such things. But ...'

Very often you see parents saying 'no' to their kids in public, either with a verbal 'no', or with some physical gesture. Nobody complains about these everyday things, but if you take a close look you see little robots being created, exactly like their parents, not given the freedom and space they need to be themselves. One very common phenomenon that lies behind this 'no' from adults is the feeling of being insecure to express what is really happening in a particular moment. Instead, they are always looking to see what is expected.

While one aspect of conscious parenting is being aware enough to give the child space from your own structures, it is usual for parents to doubt their parenting choices. We have a fourteen-year-old teenager living in the community who has been here since he was eight. His mother, Ute, was one of the first to show interest in starting a community and played an important part in making it work at the beginning. As her teenage son is becoming more independent, she worries that she didn't raise him well and that she could have done things better. She came to talk to me after she had taken him to school one morning.

When I think of him I always feel so much guilt, and I don't know how to deal with it. All the time it comes: 'I didn't do enough for him when he was small.'

Does he feel any of that, or is it only you?

It's only me; he's fine. When I ask him about it, he always says, 'I'm sorry Mum, but I don't know what you mean.' But that doesn't help me. Still I always think I didn't do enough, I didn't give him the family he wanted to have, I wasn't patient enough with him, I didn't spend enough time with him because I had to work. Sometimes it comes up that I gave too much time to my own interests. It's all part of the guilt.

But *he* doesn't feel any of that. Most sons, if they really feel pissed off with their mother, would be quite quick to say so. If he doesn't say anything about it, even when you ask him to tell you, then maybe you weren't as bad as you thought.

It's a problem because I don't trust what he says in that moment. I think maybe he is not aware of how it really was at the time. I don't know how to drop the guilt. I don't know how to come out of these thoughts. I work on it and it stops for a moment but then it comes again.

Every mother's mind has some kind of similar story running. As we look at it now I can see that it's not really true. But that doesn't help you very much because *you* don't see that.

We can only do in any moment what we can do. Now you have more wisdom than when you were twenty, so if you were raising him now, with all the experiences of life you've had in the last years, maybe you would be a much better mother. But life doesn't work like that. It is as it is. There is no perfect parent. There never has been and there never will be.

Basically, existence decides who you get. It's a lottery. Your son ended up with you and if he's not complaining you could probably guess that you did a fairly good job as a mum. You don't have any reason to feel guilty. You couldn't have done any better, and if you could have done, you would have.

Maybe you're not the very best of mothers, I don't know. I couldn't judge that, but in the workings of existence it just happens the way it happens, yes? Everyone does what they can. I don't even believe you're a 'mother' who hasn't done a good job. The fact that we are talking probably suggests you're ready to look at this possibility. We are animated by consciousness, and in a way we don't do anything. It's doing us. If you are in doubt, just love your child. If you allow some greater freedom as well, the child will be even more happy.

It takes generations for cultural conditioning to shift. Some years ago I lived in Sydney near Bondi, the world-famous surfing and sunbathing beach. It is completely beautiful, but when I walked around I was shocked by the older buildings. The whole area had originally been settled by British immigrants and despite the stunning beauty of the ocean and the beaches, they had built exactly the same little ugly boxes with tiny windows that you can see in suburban London.

We create the world in our image, the image that comes from our conditioned mind. It starts when we are very small children and is naturally supported by our parents and by the society and culture in which we live.

You know how your parents brought you up. You know where they came from because you met your grandparents and you can see the patterns that persist from generation to generation, just like British architecture persisted in Australia despite it being totally unsuitable. Changing these inherited patterns can only happen if you decide as a parent to be more conscious in how you interact with your child. This is challenging because it's much easier just to pass on to your children the conditioned behaviour you got from your parents.

I think it would be true to say that most people believe children should surrender to their parents, but my own feeling is that the parents should surrender to their children. Surrendering to the children doesn't mean running along behind them letting them do what they want, being as naughty as they like. I don't mean it like that. Of course there have to be some nurturing boundaries, but understanding that the child is not an extension of a parent's ego structure, 'my child', brings a radical change.

Ute has another son, Amrit, who was born during the first year of our community. When he was around two years old he sometimes used to sleep in my room. He would sleep in a sleeping bag suit and in the morning I would take him out of his bed and unzip him. Out would step a little Superman! In the beginning he was completely happy to play in my room. He would go and find the light switch and turn it on, turn it off, turn it on again, and so on. I wondered what he was doing but I was able to control my leave-that-light-switch-alone reaction. We would have a very nice half hour each morning and I used to look forward to this playtime with him.

Then one day he didn't want to play in my room anymore. I unzipped him and then he was out the door! Where was he going? I had this feeling, 'Play with me!' But he didn't want to play with me. He wanted to play with one of his friends in the house. He wanted to go down and have some adventures. It is very subtle. Just surrender to your child. Does it matter what he is playing around with? He is not going to do something awful.

> *Some children were lined up for lunch in the cafeteria of a Catholic kindergarten. At the head of the table was a large pile of apples. A teacher had made a note and posted it on the apple tray: 'Take only ONE. God is watching.'*
> *Moving further along the lunch line, at the other end of the table a kid had put out a large pile of chocolate chip cookies. They left a little note: 'Take all you want. God is watching the apples.'*

Amrit has been brought up by a whole bunch of people living in our community. The community's population is not completely stable and some have come and gone over the years. People he has been close to have left and new ones have come. However several have cared for him since his birth. He is also very good at choosing guests to be friends. Love seems to be the common glue to all these relationships.

There was a nice moment at his kindergarten when he was asked who his daddy was, and he replied, 'Which one?' That's getting a little more complicated as he gets older, of course, but there are some very big advantages in being brought up in a loving community. When he is being parented by different people there seems to be a levelling out: somebody is a little bit strict and then somebody else is more easy going. He is not getting just the full blast of one person's particular ego structures.

I see him as an amazing model of a possibility because he is a very well-adjusted child. He has a basically silent nature, a sense of inner peace, and with that he is able to develop as things unfold in his life. It is a joy to see how he benefits from the 'group parenting'.

A mother came to one of my meetings and was telling me that when she had her daughter she made a conscious decision that she didn't want to just pass on her mother's generation of ideas to her. She wanted to be a conscious parent. She told me that even though she had made this decision, and even though she was being vigilant, time and again she was able to see that actually she was just acting out pretty much exactly the way her mother used to act out towards her. So, what to do?

If you believe that this child is 'my' child, there's very little you can do. But if you have some sense that you are not separate, if you have some sense about the truth of who you are and who your child is, then there is another possibility. You can step back, not possess your child and not make your child into an extension of your ego. Take care that you are not holding onto your child to provide the love that is missing in your own life.

Of course there is another aspect of parenting, because children need care. You know bedtimes have to be decided and there are certain routines and behaviours that have to be taught. Important choices about schooling and health have to be made, but I would say the most important part of all that is to provide a loving environment. It is the most fertile ground in which to raise children.

The most conscious position you can take with your children is to see them not as your children but as free beings who have come to you for a limited period. You can feel humbled by the great trust in that situation.

One of the things that is so beautiful about children is an innocence, a beingness that keeps them completely absorbed in the present moment. It is so strong that before going out to play, for example, they can't imagine that outside it's raining or snowing. This is where you need an adult around who can project into the future and say, 'If you want to go out today you need an umbrella because it's raining.' Children are innocently spontaneous. With this quality of heart you don't need an umbrella; you just go outside and dance in the rain.

Basically, kids like to jump in the puddles and parents usually just think of the wet shoes and socks and 'you might get cold' and so on. The child is just there, not caring about what might or might not happen. Children live without any reason. You can also live without any reason.

My advice to anyone who wants to parent more consciously is to stand back and give the children as much space as possible. Let them discover life themselves. Children have their own intelligence and at the right time and in the right place that will naturally develop their unique understanding of life.

Chapter 5
How We Sabotage Ourselves

*We all have so many reasons to be afraid.
We can't move because of this fear.
What are all these fears about?
If you start to go into it, you'll find out
that the basic fear is always the same.
We are all interested in coming to Truth,
and yet what are we most afraid of? Truth.
And what is Truth?
It is also love and beauty and peace.
On one hand we want these things,
but on the other hand we are afraid of them.*

Chapter 5
How We Sabotage Ourselves

Life is flowing through us and we find ourselves losing touch with our old identity. We become open to life, but also we become vulnerable. The unknown mystery of life is opening, so a great fear can arise. We all have the longing to deeply meet ourselves, but at the same time it is what we most fear. We have very successful and subtle strategies to sabotage our own happiness, the meeting with our own Self. The most common is reverting to old patterns of thinking and behaviour. We fall into what we know, choosing relationships and familiar lifestyles instead of the mystery of living in the unknown.

The Prison of the Mind 137
Fear and Attachment

Structures of the Mind 144
Identification and Judgment

The Ultimate Illusion 151
Love and Relationship

Living in La La Land 160
The Effects of Trauma

The Prison of the Mind
Fear and Attachment

We have a grand piano standing in the main room of the house, where the guests from our guesthouse enter and the visitors and volunteers come to relax. The piano occupies a prime place in the centre of the room, standing by two windows that overlook the river, yet it is not played so much. Every now and again someone in the house practises or puts on a performance, but far more beautiful is when someone comes quite unexpectedly to the house and suddenly we hear the piano singing out over lunch or during a tea break.

One Sunday, a Japanese friend of a resident arrived to visit this friend and also to get some direction and guidance after going through a difficult time in her life. Her visit coincided with an art exhibition opening. She arrived very shy, and was immediately drawn to the piano.

She didn't know anyone except her friend, but she sat down anyway and started playing the most incredibly sweet music in a very professional way. The guests all enjoyed it very much, and gave her a round of applause when she had finished. It turned out that she hadn't played for some years. From her twenties onwards her life had become very busy, and then she had had a breakdown. The piano was always her passion but she had blocked it out of her life somehow.

During the whole time she stayed she was incredibly shy to play again. She didn't have a job, had lost some family members and was living in Holland, thousands of miles from home. She had a great fear and uncertainty of the future.

Some time after the impromptu concert she gave at the exhibition opening, I talked to her about her situation and what was going on for her.

How We Sabotage Ourselves

I have so much to see. This story that's happening in my life is such a big drama. Maybe it is not so big actually, but for me it's big. Everything has collapsed and I don't know what to do. I feel a lot of fear of letting go and I'm clinging to my ideas and habits and the old way that I've been acting and living my life.

This is very beautiful because you can see that it's exactly what the mind will try to do when it's faced with something unknown. It seems to me existence is giving you a big shake-up. You have to find out what that is about. You probably have many ideas about yourself that are being challenged right now.

The invitation is to really look at and enquire about the basis of these ideas: the 'me' that has them. For most of your life you probably just assumed you were a 'me' because everybody seemed to be a 'me'. It all seemed quite normal. But now something has come up that disturbs that and you feel a lot of fear.

Yes, I don't have anything left. I've completely lost myself.

Well, you lost some of the attachments, but you certainly didn't lose yourself. You were attached to the people who have left your life, and maybe you were attached to your house and your job. You were attached to a lot of things that gave you an identity. They made you feel secure. Your life was going along and you were kind of okay – gently asleep.

Yes. I was searching for something, but I was happy. Then life came and shook me up!

Suddenly you separated from your husband and you lost the house. Your sister died, and then your father. You were in Japan and then you lost your job. Now you're living in a very uncomfortable room in a foreign country with no job. So all this upheaval has given you

The Prison of the Mind

a good opportunity to examine who you are. What's important in your life? What do you want? It is a very insecure moment.

It is such a difficult time for me right now. I've got nothing to hold onto, nothing familiar.

You probably feel completely vulnerable and insecure, like you have no foundation. And in a way, this is all horrible. You feel completely like a victim of a drama you didn't want.

Yes!

Human life is full of this kind of drama. But rather than seeing it as a tragedy, try to see it as a gift. It presents a beautiful opportunity to find out what is really important to you and to see who you really are, without all the trimmings.

Yes, I can see that. Thank you.

We're happy just sleeping in the sunshine. So existence takes us, picks us up and shakes us. You have to come to this kind of hopeless moment. It has a beauty about it, even though it's very uncomfortable. Existence has taken away a lot, but, just like the tide, it will come back in again. You don't have to do anything, and you *can't* really do anything. The only thing you can do is to stay as quiet as possible so that you can make real contact with your being. Then you'll get guidance and you can move forward.

That's quite scary, because I'm not used to this part of me and I don't know where to go, or more importantly, what part of myself to follow.

We have a vacancy actually, for a piano player. We also have a vacancy in the kitchen. We've been looking for a Japanese sushi chef for a long time. So there you are – two job offers already!

How We Sabotage Ourselves

I'll think about it.

Don't think about it! If you do, you'll go crazy. Just give it some space, give it some opportunity. Life is a mystery to be lived. When it's all very comfortable and predictable it isn't so interesting. The more you invite the mystery, the more you will find the true home.

•⎯⎯⎯•

I love travelling around Europe, giving meetings and visiting all kinds of different places. I've had many meetings and met probably thousands of people. Often they come very enthusiastic and open and some kind of connection begins. For many, that seems to be all they want and after one or two evenings they don't come anymore.

Other people stay longer and become more involved. But again, very often when these people seem to be coming very close to some deep understanding, you could say coming close to awakening, they also suddenly disappear. It seems that a deep fear arises, a fear of the apparent death of the illusionary self together with the fear of the approaching emptiness.

What is this fear about? Once you begin to investigate who you think you are, the layers fall away – a bit like an onion. When you come to the centre, what do you find? Nothing. This is scary because you've always been 'somebody' and now it looks like you're 'nothing'. Which is better? Maybe it's better to be 'somebody' with wrong ideas than to be absolutely 'nothing'. But this is not as scary as it sounds because 'nothing' does not refer to a barren wasteland. It means not having a head full of ideas, not having all kinds of concepts, not having any more attachment to the old structures that have built up over many years. Being 'nothing' means being fresh, spontaneous, innocent and present.

We are all afraid of emptiness, of not existing. For the ego or false self it appears like death. That's why we 'blah, blah' all day long, to convince ourselves that we are alive, a reminder that we are not dead. It is to convince ourselves that this emptiness that we really are, this nothing that we really are, is not true.

The basic fear is always the same. We are all interested in coming to Truth, and yet what are we most afraid of? Truth. And what is Truth? It is also love and beauty and peace. On one hand we want these things, but on the other hand we are afraid of them.

Most people's lives are completely in bondage because of fear. As you come very close to the moment of awakening, basically what you realise is that everything you believe yourself to be is simply not true. You start to see this illusion, you start to understand it and you also start to see that as the illusion falls away it is a kind of death. Naturally, there's a lot of fear arising from that.

There is an assumption that if you would really let go deeply then a lot would change, and this possibility can be frightening. Either you're afraid you will lose everything you have believed yourself to be or you will lose everything on the outside. You won't be able to maintain your apartment or your job, and maybe you will lose your family.

This deep fear is a natural part of the conditioned mind and so when it arises it is a sign that the person is coming close to a true understanding. It is a natural part of the whole journey. People often sabotage themselves by moving away from Truth because of this fear. The mind is always afraid of the unknown, and it is not possible to know what will happen when you let go of the familiar. By staying identified with the fear you stay in the prison of the known, the familiar, and you can never meet Truth.

During the French Revolution, the revolutionaries stormed the Bastille and released everyone. The prisoners rushed out and shouted, 'Freedom! Vive la révolution!' But in the evening, amazingly, most of the prisoners returned to their cells. It had become their home, their own world where they felt comfortable.

I have had many moments when the fear of the unknown was strong, and it felt like coming to the edge of a cliff. There is always the choice: you can take a few steps back into the known or you can take a deep breath and jump. You never know what will happen but my experience is that life always opens up into something new and wonderful. Fear is always attached to an idea that life can be terrible, that hell is waiting if we just take the wrong step.

You have to understand fear and how it binds you. The conditioned mind believes itself to be a somebody. This somebody is afraid – afraid of this, afraid of that. We accept this fear as if it is a fact, and then we can't move because it becomes real. We can't see that this is all going on in our own minds. We are creating an idea and then being afraid of it. When you really look, it is so ridiculous. You can't even imagine you would ever do that.

The other thing I would say is that when you actually do let go and jump, the people that you need to support you appear. But there are no deals. You can't stand on the top of the cliff and say, 'Okay Existence, I will jump but first I want to know that I am going to jump into a nice place.' Unfortunately it doesn't work like that. The help you think you want isn't necessarily what will appear. There needs to be trust and acceptance of what life is actually bringing you.

> *A lost man, desperate for water, was walking through the desert when he saw something far off in the distance. Hoping to find water, he hurried towards it, only to find a little old man at a small stand selling ties.*
> *The man asked desperately, 'Do you have water?'*
> *The old man replied, 'I have no water. Would you like to buy a tie? They are only five dollars.'*
> *The man shouted, 'What the hell?! I don't need an overpriced tie you idiot! I need water, damn it!!'*
> *'Okay, okay,' said the old man, 'there's no need to get angry. If you go over that hill to the east for about two kilometres you will find a lovely, high-class restaurant. It has all the ice-cold water you need. Good luck.'*
> *Muttering, the man staggered away over the hill. Several hours later he staggered back, almost dead. 'You bastard! They won't let me in without a tie!'*

The Prison of the Mind

The mind has fear about trusting the flow of life. It fears anything new or unknown. If you really come to 'nothingness' in a profound way, then that is the end of the conditioned mind. In the nothingness, the attachment to 'me' dissolves. Over time the structures depending on this 'me' also dissolve. When we see the illusion of the mind, naturally the mind is resistant and fearful.

A mature member of our community has had a driving licence for years but had fallen into a strong fear about driving. I suggested she could deal with the fear by driving again. So first with a companion and then alone on quiet roads she managed pretty well, but still she was afraid of going on motorways. One day I needed to be driven to a doctor and she was the only one available. I offered my car and we set off. It involved several motorways and she managed very well. Now her old fear has dissolved.

Taking a step towards fear is the only way to see its illusory nature. As you step towards it you will find that something is liberated. And if you step very often towards your fears, you'll find that they can't hold you in the same way anymore. It also gives you the chance to see that the mechanism of fear is the fear of the unknown, the unknowable. It is fear of just being here now, in this peaceful nothing.

Structures of the Mind
Identification and Judgment

Every year at the end of July we host an arts festival in the community. We offer workshops in dance, theatre, music, painting and sculpture, with the evenings free for Satsang, concerts and space to come inside. It's always a spicy mix of different kinds of people, and it usually feels like a travelling circus has come to town. Our six-year-old boy, Amrit, loves this time of the year, because along with all his usual playmates in the community he has an extra bunch of wacky characters milling around.

It's very beautiful because he doesn't have so many judgments about people, so he engages with more or less any kid or adult who comes into the house. He doesn't say, 'Well, I don't like little girls,' or 'I don't like this guy, he's too old.'

Maybe when he starts to play with them he discovers certain things are not really possible with that person; but he doesn't really care. He just has the most fun he can with that person in that moment, because he doesn't have all the adult judgments. He's empty. He's quiet. He's not in a story. He's spontaneous, innocent and in the moment.

During the festival I had been talking about recognising the separate false self inside, about seeing its patterns and judgments running along. Stefan, one of the participants, had been playing with Amrit almost the whole festival, whenever there was time, and I think he had been deeply touched by the spontaneity and joy he had discovered being with him.

Structures of the Mind

Recently I was contemplating this entity, this individual, this 'me'. At one point I just had to laugh because I saw, 'Hey, there's this supposed entity asking all these questions that are coming from something hallucinatory. How can the questions have any value?' Playing with Amrit showed me that.

Well, the mind does all kinds of strange stuff all the time, but one of the things it loves doing most is asking questions. However, when it gets an answer it immediately produces another question.

Part of this process that you may have already touched on is that when you have a closer understanding of who you are, the questions disappear. When we start we have many, many questions, but gradually they disappear, even if they're not really answered. They're just not relevant anymore.

Yes. My focus is narrowed down to the body-mind so everything that comes up from the body-mind is seen. It comes up, and then it can go.

The thoughts will still come, but when you're not identified with them they just go. Like clouds in the sky. They will appear and disappear, and there's no problem in it. The problem is our identification.

Yes! That's it!

Once that identification is seen through, then our stories don't grab us anymore.

When the emotions, the thoughts and the hectic situations are coming up I want to believe them, but now I can say, 'I know this is not true.' I put it away, but it still tries! It's very persistent sometimes.

Yes, there are going to be times when you will be lost in the storms, where you can't do anything because you are just 'taken'. Storms will be less and less. Some patience is needed.

Being western, we would like to have it all easy and we'd like to

How We Sabotage Ourselves

have it all *now*. We've lost the qualities of patience and perseverance. If you want to be a master craftsman you have to surrender to the process of learning how to really deal with the tools and the materials. This takes many years of training and experience. What you're talking about, for you, seems absolutely lovely. Perfect.

If I just close my eyes and get really quiet and try to leave all the concepts alone, the mind becomes very subtle. It always wants to create something to engage with. I can't even tell what it is sometimes. It just makes some kind of picture, 'This is the way it's supposed to be!'

What you're describing is totally honest. It's very, very subtle, and it's so sensitive that we can't even always see it. It requires a very sharp self-awareness.

Yes, that's right. But there's also a little part that says, 'Ah! Later on. First I'm going to do this and then that…' It just wants to wriggle around and not feel that silence, like it's postponing going into real silence.

It depends, from mind to mind, but yes, the mind is always sabotaging. Something else we could say about it is that fear can arise. The mind wants to exist but in Satsang we're rubbing away the identification, which will lead to stillness. The mind will potentially freak out because it fears its own death, its own destruction.

It isn't the death of the organism; it is the death of a false idea. While we think our ideas are real, while we are identified with the mind, we can become very fearful as we come closer and closer to the sense of it all ending. That's why being with people who understand what is happening to you is very supportive. In the energy of Satsang it is just naturally easier to be still.

I think everybody reading this understands that we are not the ego, the false self. We know it, but it's almost impossible to live it because

Structures of the Mind

we are caught up with all kinds of structures of the mind. Things that started when we were very small and defenceless have accumulated. We were innocent, absorbing whatever was happening, and the effect of this over many years is that we've completely fallen in love with the wrong me. We've fallen in love with the story, which we absolutely believe and which is constantly fed back to us. By examining the structures of our minds we get to see who we are *not*.

Our minds are continuously repeating familiar patterns that we've come to describe as 'me'. That's why, in the end, it's very difficult to live what is an extremely simple Truth. The Truth is so simple it hardly even needs talking about. You all know it just as clearly as I know it, but how to live it?

The structured mind is not so different from person to person. Generally speaking, men's minds are more often busy with their inner judgments and women's with their emotions. These are the sabotage mechanisms we have learned to use to *not* look at the apparent nothingness. By being preoccupied with judgments and emotions we can't feel our beingness. We avoid our fear of simply being quiet, silent.

Some time ago we had a rather splendid actress living in our community and she was able to create a drama out of almost anything. As I got closer to her I could see that the trigger was not that anything particular was happening; it was that *nothing* was happening. Nothing happening was the trigger for her to create an emotional cloud. She was doing that to avoid herself. Men do it with their judgments. Of course there are also women who have a strong judgmental side and men who have a strong emotional side.

It is necessary to remember the possibility of simply being present with whatever is happening. Stay with it, even if it is uncomfortable and the mind is judging and reacting. We have ideas of how it should be and what we like; we are all moving away from this moment, moving towards some hypothetical better deal that is just around the corner. Whether the mind is judging what is happening as good or bad, just stay with it. By staying with it for a short time there is a possibility to come through to silence.

How We Sabotage Ourselves

When you are really content, with a relaxed knowing, then you are not so dramatic or emotional. Identifying with your emotions and judgments is a very strong sabotage because it gives energy to exactly what you don't want to give energy to. You want to give it to the silence and the nothingness: to who you really are. If you want to hold onto the emotions and judgments, fine, but your life will be full of suffering.

As you go deeper you can begin to see that all your actions are motivated by the patterns or structures in your mind. You appear to be free. You can go anywhere you like for a holiday, so in that limited way you can say you are free. Yet what about in a deeper way? When you start to look diligently you find out that you are a prisoner of your programming. It's not always easy to see this programming because it feels so natural.

If you start to look deeper inside yourself, you can begin to see the motives for some of your actions. Here is an example of how the energy can be misdirected. One of our residents always sat quietly cross-legged with his eyes closed when everyone else was dancing. He looked very spiritual. When he honestly examined this behaviour he found that actually he was afraid of dancing and he had a strong judgment about other people dancing. He thought they looked silly, and he applied that judgment to himself as well. He didn't want to appear silly while dancing so he avoided the situation by apparently meditating.

I am not saying it was wrong to sit and it would be right to dance. It doesn't matter either way. What I am saying is that if you watch these structures you can gradually get a sense that you are not free and that in fact you are a prisoner of your programming. Awakening means to awaken out of the programming.

It is very easy to see the extent of other people's structures. Looking at your own, however, is a different story entirely because you already have set ideas about yourself. There are structures where you couldn't even imagine they could be. Many of them are so subtle that you wouldn't even call them a structure. Perhaps you are ready to admit, 'Okay, maybe I can change some of the difficult, nasty structures into nicer, friendlier ones. Then things will be okay.' It doesn't hurt to shift some of the things that don't work so well in your life, but it doesn't make much difference. You can be just as attached to nice structures as you can to nasty ones.

My own feeling is that when you investigate more deeply and you begin to grasp the extent of the structures, you can choose to completely give up. When you make a judgment – 'I like this, but I *don't* like that' – you're empowering your false self to continue running this separate, false story: 'my life'.

So the invitation is to completely surrender and just say 'yes'. Notice how that feels inside. 'Oh, it's raining today. I'll get my umbrella.' Accept everything as it is, in every moment of your life. Again, that's extremely simple but almost impossible to do. You can make a commitment, 'Okay, I'm just going to say "yes".' Then ten minutes later when somebody asks you, 'Can you go and clean the toilet?' 'No! I don't do toilets!' And so it goes on.

Over the last days I have experienced agonising back pain. I never really have any health problems except this pain that comes once a year for about five days. Despite the intensity of the pain, I realise nothing is really happening. Maybe tomorrow morning I'll be dead but actually right now I'm here. It makes me realise how delicate life is and I don't want to postpone anymore. Why leave freedom until later?

> *A general noticed one of his soldiers behaving oddly. The soldier would pick up any piece of paper he found, frown and say, 'That's not it,' and put it down again.*
> *This went on for some time, until the general arranged to have the soldier psychologically tested. The psychologist concluded that the soldier was deranged, and wrote out his discharge from the army.*
> *The soldier picked it up, smiled and said, 'That's it.'*

Why do you want to drag your dirty old rotten stuff along with you? It can be stepped out of. What is important in your life? If you are reading this, freedom must be important to you. So why postpone what you can do right now? Actually there is nothing to do. You just have to be very clear about what is really you and what is not you.

You are behaving from many deeply held structures that you totally believe are necessary for survival. It is not true! The belief in these structures is exactly what is keeping you from what you most want – the Self.

Find out what doesn't change. Find out what is constant, what has always been here. It doesn't matter what we are doing on the outside. It doesn't matter what the thoughts are. It doesn't matter what we feel, or what the structures are. What is here all the time is awareness being aware of what we are feeling, what we are thinking, what we are doing. This awareness is constant.

The Ultimate Illusion
Love and Relationship

As I am writing this, Marianne, a woman who lives in our community, is taking a break from her time here and trying to find out what her priorities in life are. She is a very lovely woman who has lived with us for three years, much loved by everybody, but has become very much caught up in one love story after the other.

When I was starting out on my path of self-discovery I had a beautiful Japanese wife. Her dream was that we would have a nice little house, unpack all our boxes of treasures and live together happily ever after. I was keen for this too, but after a few years of living happily ever after I said to her, 'I'm sorry, but I have to go back to my spiritual master.' And she said, 'Well – that's a bit difficult for me! So I'll stay here and you go to your master.' And then we left each other, very sweetly, with love. It was not an easy moment for me. I had no reason to leave her and twenty years later we are still friends. But she had other priorities in her life. I respected her priorities, she respected mine and the flow of life took us apart.

In that way, Truth is completely uncompromising. You can compromise your priority, of course. That's always an option, and it's very easy to choose that. A strong compromise is to choose a love affair. Rather than Truth, you choose a wife, a husband, a lover.

This is what I wanted to help Marianne with, as it looked like she was compromising herself in exactly this way. Even though she was open to looking at her situation, in the end she was choosing the love affair rather than awakening. She had such a strong desire to be with a man and to create some kind of family story. So now she has gone away for a month to really look at this issue. Before she went, I had a talk with her about her situation and the key that she wasn't seeing.

How We Sabotage Ourselves

There was always this wish for happiness and deep love, which I projected onto finding a man. It's what I was told: 'You find love with a man.' But I can see that it's not like that, because the happiness and the love that I feel always depend on whether the relationship is working or not working.

I think this comes from the little girl inside you, the unconscious structure of your mind that was put there when you were small, living in a family that perhaps wasn't so happy. This little girl got the idea at that time that if she lived in a 'happy family' she could be happy. Do you see that?

Yes. But then it's so hard to believe that if I really want to wake up I have to give up my desire for relationship.

And any other strong desire – until the longing to awaken is your last longing. Otherwise, inevitably, you will go to that other desire. In order to awaken, you have to come to a point where there is no hope that the 'world' is going to make you happy. You try chocolate. You try ice cream. You try a car, a house. You try a girlfriend, a boyfriend. You try all these different things, but you have to finish with all desire, all 'wanting' and 'getting'. What is going on now?

I don't know, exactly. It's just that there's so much pain. I can see that for my whole life I've been running away from the fact that I am responsible for my own happiness. I try to find so many excuses – in different ways, situations or relationships.

Can you see the possibility that if you really stop running away you'll be left with 'you'? The real 'you'!

Yes. That's right.

So although it might seem a bit terrifying, it's actually very beautiful. 'I don't need more ice cream. I don't need more red sports cars. I don't need more men. I am the Self. I am enough as I am. I am whole and complete. I don't need anything.' The only thing that can satisfy you is 'you', the authentic, real 'you'. That doesn't mean you don't get anything, but there comes a moment when you can say: 'No thank you. I don't need it.' Why do you need something? You are whole and complete. What's missing right now?

Nothing. Not really. It's so to the point, what you say: there is no hope.

There is no hope. And if there is hope, then you just go off chasing that hope. (Silence)

I'm shocked!

That's good.

Love is an energy phenomenon centred around the point we associate with the heart, in the middle of the chest. As that energy centre becomes open we find that we are able to experience love with everybody and with all of existence. This is unconditional love, because it is not from the mind. This is the love that simply manifests, simply bubbles up and overflows.

The human tragedy is that almost no one knows this. Everyone feels a lack of love. We are always looking for it and we always look in the wrong place. The mistaken idea that we are missing something causes most of us to live in suffering. We suffer because of completely wrong ideas. One is the fundamental misunderstanding that each of us is a somebody and we are trying to relate with another somebody.

Another mistaken idea is that we believe we're missing something. Everybody is trying to find the missing bit. Who is keeping us from our true nature? Only us. We are doing it to ourselves. It's a tragic situation and actually the solution is very simple. Incredibly simple. The solution is to do nothing, because then there is simply authentic love. It's always there, like a spring flowing from the hillside. Every kind of doing takes you away from that.

The main way you keep yourself from Truth is through relationship with something or someone; we could call this the ultimate illusion. You have a relationship with the world in which you are separate from all those objects out there. You have a relationship with somebody and pretty soon you are not only caught up in your own life story (like an illusionary movie script), but also in their life story and then, of course, quite quickly in 'our' relationship story.

Even living only with 'my' story we are completely lost because we believe I'm somebody who is separate from everything. We are trying desperately to relate with everything because we're trying to find union, become one. When we go into relationship with somebody we now have their story to manage as well as the story of the relationship. So instead of one story, now there are three stories. I would be ready to stick my neck out and say there isn't one relationship in the whole world that really works. By its very nature it can't. This illusion keeps us from our true nature.

How can you become quiet when you have all these stories going on? You believe this person is giving you love and if they hug or smile at somebody else you feel jealous because you think there is going to be less love for you. The basis of jealousy is a complete misunderstanding about love. Romantic love is possessive. We become jealous because 'my' partner is loving another.

When you find out who you are, you relate with everything – but there is no relationship because now you know that you are one with everything. You know you are not separate and therefore there is no question of relationship. The whole game of relationship is a game of two separates trying to become one. It can't work. You can try it with every beautiful woman or man, even with your perfect soul mate; it will never work.

The romantic love of Hollywood epics and pop songs is everywhere, dripping off everything in society – the wonderful romance of 'falling in love'. This is not the love I am talking about, but rather love as an energy phenomenon. It is simply the love that wells up and spills over in the heart chakra. This love is similar to the water gushing out of a spring in the hillside. It gushes whether or not someone drinks from it. This is unconditional love.

Falling in love is the ultimate illusion, because to fall in love there must be somebody who falls in love with somebody else – me and you. And, as we know, when there is me and you then I am identified with 'my life'. This brings many dramas, stories, beliefs, desires and longings. This is all part of being somebody.

Your life energy is caught up with sorting out all these stories, and if you are lucky a little bit of love happens. If you are unlucky you will be unhappy and miserable. Somewhere in the distance – at the end of the rainbow – is love, but you never quite find it. However much effort you put in, it always seems just a little further away. Falling in love is packaged so nicely that it's easy to believe it.

When we were very small we were totally dependent on whoever was taking care of us. We were in their hands; our survival depended on them. So in that situation we developed strategies to do with survival in terms of getting the love and nourishment that we needed. Those strategies have stayed with us, locked into our psychology.

Many of us developed a wound that gradually appeared as low self-esteem. It came out of the fact that when we were small we were not validated for who we actually were but were made to feel that our survival depended on certain actions towards whoever was looking after us, usually our parents. This wound manifests in different ways, but fundamentally as a sense of need. We feel we are not complete; something is missing. That thing that we need to get we call 'love'. I want to be loved, I need to be loved, I am looking for a lover.

So we look around outside ourselves until we meet somebody with whom we have a certain chemistry. Then we attract that person and we feel him or her bringing us love. Momentarily we feel very good because now we feel complete. We have found someone who provides us with the nourishment to heal our wounds.

But unfortunately, that person may choose to go away. So we

How We Sabotage Ourselves

always fear that the love that is so nicely filling up the wound and nourishing us may go away. We develop strategies to keep that love. Some of the strategies are from our past and some are quite new, but together they are all designed to keep this person and the love that we think we need.

We become possessive and jealous, living in the fear of being abandoned or rejected. We have all experienced those particular issues at some time. We all know how powerful they are, how much we are affected by them. They all come from the fear that the love we feel we need to fill our wound may go away. Then, of course, if this happens we are back with the wound. For some time it had been healed and suddenly it is there again, so it can seem that the pain is even greater.

The actual Truth is that we are already complete. Knowing who we are will totally heal the wound. Then any relating is there to simply enjoy the play, not because we think we need to be nourished. The whole quality of relating changes.

> *A friend asked a gentleman how it is that he never married? Replied the gentleman, 'Well, I guess I just never met the right woman. I guess that I have been looking for the perfect girl.'*
> *'Oh, come on now,' said the friend, 'Surely you have met at least one girl that you wanted to marry.'*
> *'Yes, there was a girl, once. I guess she was the one perfect girl, the only perfect girl I really ever met. She was just the right everything. I really mean that she was the perfect girl for me,' replied the gent.*
> *'Well, why didn't you marry her?' asked his friend.*
> *The gent replied, 'She was looking for the perfect man.'*

Expecting and hoping that the other is going to give you sufficient love to heal your wound is a business arrangement, and it compromises real love. While you are living in the belief that the other is going to love you then nothing true can ever happen. There's nothing wrong in having a nice partner, but it's not going to bring you to the ultimate state of peace.

The Ultimate Illusion

What actually happens is something like this: you meet somebody and for some reason you look at this person and you think, 'Oh, wow!' And in this 'Wow!' your mind stops, because you feel really touched. In that moment you're not going to start thinking about what happened last week or about the phone bill you have to pay. You're there! You're really 'be here now'. Without realising it, you're sitting there like a Buddha, very empty and present, and all this lovely stuff starts happening. Actually, this is your own love you're experiencing because your mind has stopped and you are actually being your essence.

Then you make the mistake of thinking this love has something to do with the other person. He's sitting on the other side of the table and if he has the same 'Wow!' you can end up spending the rest of your lives together. Which is okay, but what's really happening is because of this 'Wow!' It's because your mind has stopped.

These love affairs nearly always end up in lots of pain, and when we have experienced enough of this pain, when things have become completely hopeless, then we may be ready to look inside. As soon as you start looking inside, you can find out that you are not 'somebody', that it is a wrong idea and is the basic reason for all the pain. This is a very important moment. You are no longer interested in relating outside and you *are* interested in relating inside.

Your whole focus shifts. Instead of looking for somebody out there to bring you love – which is missing – you can look inside and find out that you *are* love and that nothing is missing, that in fact you are whole and complete and that you don't need to 'get' anything. Then you can relax.

Everything changes. There is just love, piles of love, and it is available for everybody, not just for the people with the same ideas as you or for those special friends who signed the paper. This love is unconditional and has no boundaries. It doesn't depend on what the other one is doing. It is not a business; it is not possessive. It is an overwhelming outpouring.

Make the relationship with yourself the focus of your life. Out of that relationship will come all other relationships, and suddenly,

How We Sabotage Ourselves

for the first time, it's working. Possessiveness and jealousy simply drop away because the fear of being abandoned is no longer present. You can accept the person being there, you can accept the person leaving. It's not such a big deal anymore because you are complete in yourself. That is the difference and that is what makes it work.

Authentic love is very rare, because you must first wake up from the illusion that you are somebody with a story, seeing and relating to the world from 'I'. When you wake up from this illusion you are ready for authentic love. You don't have to do anything. You *are* the authentic love. There is no question about falling in love; love is just happening and available.

Over the years this is what I have tried to explain to Marianne, encouraging her to look deeply into her own experience.

I can see that what it all comes down to is this desire for love and freedom and peace.

But the love and the peace does not come from somebody else. It is your nature! The love and happiness and peace are your own nature.

Yes, I understand this. I heard this, okay?

Yes, but you haven't only heard it, Marianne. You have even experienced it! Do you remember that Sunday morning?

Yes, for sure.

What happened first?

What happened?

Come on. You got out of bed and you came to the meditation. It was like any other Sunday morning, but something happened, right?

Yes. It was like a huge opening. It was like falling deep, deep down into myself.

What did you find there?

A lot of joy! And happiness!

Happiness?!

Yes!

So you didn't find vats of burning oil and dragons and devils?

No. I was very surprised that there was such beauty and so much peace.

Tell me again! You see, this was *you*, Marianne! It did not come to you from your boyfriend, the perfect man for you. It did not come from anybody, not even from Premananda. It was coming from *you*! Don't forget this. That's you!

It's interesting to see how powerful is society's conditioning about the happy family. Even though Marianne has had a strong taste several times of the happiness welling up from inside her, she is still resolute in her attempts to find happiness through the pursuit of the perfect man.

She comes from a family where she and her sister were regularly abused by their father, while her mother failed to intercede. Her own relationships have all failed and she is left to care for two children. Despite all this she still carries the fantasy of the happy family being the answer to all her longings.

Living in La La Land
The Effects of Trauma

When I am being with myself there is just presence, and there is nothing to take me away from presence. When working with people in the community they often seem present, but when I probe a little deeper into their experience I find that they are somewhere else, running on autopilot without presence or even awareness that they are not present.

Recently I arrived back at the house after an outing to find a plant with withered leaves welcoming me at the front door, the same front door used by every guest of the guesthouse and every other visitor to Open Sky House. When I approached Carol, the woman whose responsibility it is to look after the upkeep of the house, she said she hadn't noticed it before. I couldn't help but be shocked as it was clear that she simply wasn't present.

The day after my heated talk with her, Carol wrote me an email explaining what she was experiencing. I read it out in Satsang, and my response was not only for her but for everyone who was listening.

I find myself walking around the house in 'la la land'. I heard you call it that once before, but I don't understand what is going on when I'm in it. I can see the room around me and feel that I'm thinking a bit, but my being feels totally absent. Something inside doesn't want to be present, and the whole feeling has a background of discomfort and some kind of pain or ache in my body. I feel stuck and frustrated, but don't know how to come out of it.

I started meditation to try and become more aware, and I

understand about patience, because some things have changed a lot since I started meditating. But the dozy state of 'la la land' is really strong in my life and I can't see exactly what causes it.

Sometimes I can see it when it comes over me, but then I get angry because I expect it to go away once I have seen it, but it doesn't. So it feels like I'm 'suffering consciously'…which is clearly frustrating. Above all I hate it that I'm not there for my life as it's happening. Instead I'm stuck in a dream world, protecting myself against I don't know what. Can you say something about what's happening in 'la la land', this default position I often adopt in life? And can you also suggest how I can come out of it?

What I mean by 'la la land' is an on-going situation where you are not present; your attention and focus are somewhere else. It's a place where you don't have to feel whatever it is you don't want to feel. You just leave the body. When I look around this meeting, you all look like you're here. Some of you have your eyes closed, but I'm guessing you're listening. Most of you have your eyes open and you seem to be attentive. If this were a public meeting in a city I had never been to before, then I wouldn't be thinking at all about 'la la land'. I would be taking you all as absolutely conscious, present and listening to everything I was saying – but that is not the case here and wouldn't be the case in any public meeting.

I wonder how many of you are really here right now. Probably half of you are somewhere else. It took me many years to discover this, and of course, as a teacher, it's not something I really want to discover because I'd like to imagine you're all on the edge of your chairs, listening to every word that's being spoken! Gradually, over the years of teaching, I've discovered that 'la la land' is quite a common condition, and people have it to a greater or lesser extent.

If you didn't have it at all you would be living spontaneously from moment to moment and you would be present for your life. If you're really honest, you have probably become aware yourself that you're often not present. It's actually very, very difficult to just be here. It is probably one of a human being's greatest challenges.

How We Sabotage Ourselves

We imagine, 'Of course I'm listening! Of course I heard what he said! Of course I was sitting in the room!' We imagine that we are always present for our lives, but is it true? If I really wanted to be shocking, I would say we're almost never present.

I would say there are two main reasons why we are not present. The first is the most subtle and can be difficult for people to understand. Basically, we are absolutely caught up with an idea of being a separate somebody, an actor on the stage of life. We believe this false idea of separation, this false, illusory self. When we're acting out from this character, we're not very present. We may think we are present, but we're not really. Most of our time is spent in a kind of normal 'not-being-here' because we are so caught up in our illusion.

For example, you wake up in the morning, the thinking mind ignites itself and you start paying attention to it. The day to come unfolds in your head – the worries, the doubts, the positives, the negatives, the questions, the possible answers, solutions, plans. It's endless, and it doesn't allow you to be simply present. The entire day can be spent following the movements of the mind, with minimal presence. Before you know it, you've got out of bed, washed, had breakfast and are driving at one hundred and twenty kilometres per hour down the motorway. Life becomes automated and lacks spontaneity and presence.

It's only since I've lived in the community and could observe some of the residents over several years that I have discovered the second reason for visits to 'la la land'. Let me give you an example.

I recently gave a task to Sarah, one of our newer residents. It involved commitment, time, persistence and energy to see it through to completion. In the process of doing this task she often had fits of anger and irrational judgments and she would storm out of the office, even if nothing apparently had happened. She would always blame it on someone's behaviour or the difficulty of the task, and is seemed to be impossible to talk to her and guide her to look at why she was reacting in such a strong way. She simply couldn't hear that she probably had something going on inside her, something she was not aware of that was attached to the past and that she didn't want to see.

Living in La La Land

When I asked her why there had been no movement on her task she burst out in anger and became completely defensive, firing back excuses at whatever was suggested to her. Sitting together with the whole community, I tried to address what was going on.

• ——— •

It's very hard for you to just be here. I don't know exactly what the story is but I think when you were about three years old your parents were suddenly killed in an accident.

Four years old.

For a little girl of four that would have been a huge trauma. My sense is it's still kind of vibrating inside you and it prevents you being able to focus, to be present or to go deeper into things. It was very strong.

Yes, it was. Of course.

It would have been a huge shock to your very small energy field and incredibly painful. Were you the youngest in a very big family?

Yes, there were many other brothers and sisters around.

You suffered an enormous trauma and my guess is you need to look into it in order to deal with it and move into a more mature way of living.

I don't have the feeling that it is a big issue for me. Most of the time I have the feeling I'm happy.

Maybe you are happy, but you are not here. You're happy but you're gone, and unfortunately you don't have much awareness about yourself. Although you love this place very much, you never listen to anything we try to point out to you.

No. I can't.

We are trying to give you some useful information that could be very important for you. People find it impossible to work with you in the office because you don't hear them. In the end they just give up. You have an incredibly arrogant attitude that you know and they don't.

When I'm completely caught up in it and can't see it, how can I break out of it?

The first step would be to drop the arrogance that you know everything and be much more humble. You would gradually get some feedback that you could use to understand what's going on with you. Then perhaps things could change. Over the months, people's experience of trying to relate to you is that they can't get anything into your letterbox. In the end they don't even try to send you any letters because you are in 'la la land'; you're not really here.

It's not a judgment about you as you. It's simply about how you function or don't function. Before I came to live in a community I knew hardly anything about traumas. Now I see there are many people who had some kind of very strong shock when they were small. It was so painful that the only way a small being could deal with it was to leave the body. As a result, when you become an adult it's very hard to be present.

In your case, the message that's beamed out is something like, 'Leave me alone! Leave me alone! Leave me alone!' It is a response to the pain you suffered when you were four years old, but the message persists even though now you are much older.

Yes, I can identify this feeling! 'Leave me alone, it's too painful. I don't want that – go away!'

This was probably the only strategy available to you when you were four years old, but it's not a good strategy anymore. If it continues you might end up living your life very much alone, which probably you don't want.

But why was it painful when people were close to me? I gave the message 'Leave me alone, it's too painful,' but why?

'Leave me alone' was not really directed at the people around you – it was directed at you. The pain was too much for your little system and to leave the pain you left your body.

Now you are thirty-five years old and you are still leaving your body, still leaving the pain. It is triggered by situations when you can't really hide it anymore.

Yes, I begin to see what's happening, but how to come out of it?

Your reaction was completely understandable and there's nothing personal against you. But unless you can see it and accept it, there is no chance of a healing. The first step is to become self-aware. You can't be free of something that you don't even know exists.

We see ourselves as the body and the mind, but that's not a true understanding of the human organism. You could see the mind-body entity as a vehicle, a bit like a motorcar that 'you' get in and drive. It's as if we are 'in' our bodies. There is an intimate relationship between the body and 'me', but I am not the body.

However, when we are small there is unlikely to be any awareness of this. The same emotional or physical abuse when we're grown up isn't really a problem. We can take it, to some degree at least. When we're very small we simply can't bear the pain of abuse or tragedy. We can't absorb what's going on, and so there is an automatic overdrive that takes us away – we leave the body.

Since we still carry this mechanism as adults, something dramatic or painful can be enough of a trigger to put us back into the memory of that trauma and cause us to leave the body. Even less dramatic things like having too many emails in your inbox can make you escape into 'la la land', the place where you don't have to feel whatever it is you don't want to feel. It's possible to go through the whole day in 'la la land' without anyone around you noticing that you are not present. It's only when someone has more intimate contact with you and they don't really get an expected response that they ask themselves what's going on.

Pretty much everybody has some kind of trauma. Some people in the community have been able to track back to the moment of the trauma, maybe not always with complete consciousness or awareness, but with some kind of energetic recognition of a situation that happened when they were small.

If you want to do this kind of work you need to be guided by somebody who is trained. The natural mechanism of our psychology is to block out a trauma. You don't want to go there, so you put an impenetrable concrete slab inside your psychology. You simply can't remember it.

It is not something that we really want to accept. We have a very strong conditioning that says, 'I'm okay! I'm alright!' We don't really want to look that deeply. If there are recurring situations that you find very uncomfortable, then I would say this is the time to at least be aware of slipping into 'la la land'. Something is uncomfortable, and 'Whoosh!' – you leave!

> *Seventy-year-old George went for his annual physical. All of his tests came back with normal results. Dr Smith said, 'George, everything looks great physically. How are you doing mentally and emotionally? Are you at peace with yourself, and do you have a good relationship with your God?'*
> *George replied, 'God and me are tight. He knows I have poor eyesight, so he's fixed it so that when I get up in the middle of the night to go to the bathroom, poof! the light goes on when I pee, and then poof! the light goes off when I'm done.'*

> *'Wow,' commented Dr Smith, 'that's incredible!' A little later in the day Dr Smith called George's wife. 'Thelma,' he said, 'George is just fine. Physically he's great. But I had to call because I'm in awe of his relationship with God. Is it true that he gets up during the night and poof! the light goes on in the bathroom, and then poof! the light goes off?'*
> *Thelma exclaimed, 'That old fool! He's peeing in the refrigerator again!'*

If you want to wake up, these traumas are not going to be a hindrance. You can still wake up. You can wake up right now; it takes only a moment. But if you want to live this awakening, if you want to live in freedom, then you are going to have to deal with them. It is possible that after an awakening something can trigger a trauma and everything closes down again. So if you want to live in freedom you have to look at this inner situation.

I remember after ten years of doing what you could call spiritual work, meditating mainly, I came to see that I had a structure that was afraid of life. I didn't really understand it because my memory of my parents was that I actually liked them and everything seemed pretty good. Then I discovered the importance of being born in 1944, just at the end of the Second World War.

When I was born I lived with my mother. My father was a doctor and he was away, busy in the war. I'm pretty sure that when I was very small my mother had a lot of fear about the situation. She'd lost her first husband three or four years before, when she was very young. When she was pregnant and when I was in my first year or two, she must have felt very afraid at times. Fear would also have been in the collective consciousness and transmitted through radio and newspapers.

Gradually I had the sense that the fear that I felt in certain situations was triggering some old memory of whatever had been going on when I was very small. In certain situations I can get shaky, but the difference now from say thirty years ago is that there is an awareness about it. Although it sometimes still grabs me, it is seen fairly quickly.

How We Sabotage Ourselves

So the first step is to investigate and find out for yourself. Once you expose the trauma then a natural healing begins. Awareness brings a healing, but the true way to come out of it is to wake up. As soon as you wake up there is no longer the attachment to a separate me. If there is no attachment to a separate me, then there is nothing in the psychology where you can say, 'I was traumatised,' and there's no one to slip unconsciously into 'la la land'. There may be trauma, but it is not something that I am attached to anymore. I am simply present.

Chapter 6
Reminders to Stay Present

*What is real can best be discovered
by being silent.
Just Being Quiet, we fall inside.
Tremendous peace,
tremendous oneness,
and tremendous inner nourishment.
Then, there is this void,
the Self, God, Consciousness.
We are not separate from that.
Just Be Quiet.
And there you are.*

Chapter 6
Reminders to Stay Present

Even with a fairly quiet mind and an open heart, we can still experience that being present is not so easy. The greatest pointer to presence is simply to be quiet and find what is behind the mind, what is your true nature. This requires a strong focus and a decision to really stop and not touch the old thoughts any more. Above all, we can practise Self-enquiry, constantly questioning the 'I' that we always relate to in our lives. Self-enquiry is a powerful device because it questions the core of the false identification, the 'I'.

Rubbing Out the Doodles 171
Who Am I? The Value of Self-Enquiry

The King's Banquet 179
Self-Enquiry Opens Us to Freedom

Be Quiet 186
Leaving the Stories and Coming to Peace

The Importance of 'Thank You' 195
Life is a Mirror

Rubbing out the Doodles
Who am I? The Value of Self-Enquiry

We have a little boy in the community who was born here six years ago and is now jokingly called the boss. He is full of life and innocence, really a blessing for everyone. Anyway, he was in my room recently and he showed me a new toy. It was a flat pad with two dials, which you can turn and make lines and shapes. The great bit is that when I had finished drawing something he told me to rub it out. There was another lever that you pull across the pad and it rubs out all that you have created. It hit me very strongly in that moment that Self-enquiry is wonderfully similar to this process of 'rubbing out'. While the child's toy rubs out the messy little doodles we make, leaving a blank page, Ramana Maharshi's Self-enquiry rubs out the messy little stories, taking the mind back to its source.

Ramana Maharshi – 1879 to 1950 – has become one of the twentieth century's most renowned Indian saints. He lived almost his whole life at Arunachala, a sacred mountain south of Chennai, where he went after his spontaneous Self-realisation at age sixteen in 1896. He has become famous for his simple, devotional life and his re-introduction of the ancient human question, 'Who am I?'

> *Always keeping the mind fixed in Self alone is called Self-enquiry.*
>
> Ramana Maharshi

What does Ramana mean by this? He means that you keep your awareness on your inner experience at all times. If you do this you will gradually become aware of your thoughts, your reactions, your behaviour patterns and mind structures. In particular you will see where your thoughts arise from and you will begin to understand the ego structures; you start to see your movie. He is saying that if you can go behind the mind to the source of the mind then your whole life can be lived from the source rather than from the mind. This will transform your life.

In the community, when any resident is particularly stuck in an old story and can't find a way to see clearly what is happening, I always remind them to continue Self-enquiry.

On the same day as playing with the doodle pad I was having lunch with a resident at a peaceful spot in our courtyard next to a small fishpond, where only the simple sounds of trickling water and the breeze could disturb us. This resident already had an understanding of all the basics of Self-enquiry. She had recently come into a very beautiful space from this enquiry, this simple remembering. She had come to emptiness – her true nature. However, something strong had happened that triggered an old drama and pulled her back into all the mucky stuff she had slid out of through Self-enquiry.

I've had the experience of coming into pure consciousness, or simply being. Now I find myself completely stuck in where I was before. What is this? What is consciousness?

In essence, this consciousness is always present; it never changes. The body comes; the body goes. If you identify with the body, then 'you' come and go. If you don't identify with the body, if you understand on a more absolute level, then nobody comes and nobody goes. For example, I don't see myself as an 'I', and I have no interest about where I'm going or if I'm going. Consciousness is. This 'stuff', consciousness, is the source of life. Everything around us comes from the source. We are not separate from that.

But still, you can experience feelings!

Yes. I get angry, but I don't suffer. I experience all the same things that anybody else does: maybe sadness or frustration, but there's nobody being sad and there's nobody being frustrated.

It seems that you are something that is experiencing that emotion. So you are here, experiencing it, but who are you? I still can't answer this question, who am I? Yet I am here and experiencing things.

Yes. That's a very good observation. Now you can go into it deeper and ask yourself who is experiencing it.

I think that's a big step. It's a long way to go.

No, it's not a long way to go. It's a very short way, almost no distance. It's only a trick of the mind that makes it seem a long way.

The mind is also a part of life, part of the one who experiences.

Well, you think it is. You believe you're a separate person, 'I', but is that really true?

This 'I' can experience or see my own thoughts.

Well, are they 'your' thoughts? Or are they just thoughts?

They are just thoughts, but there is someone who is thinking them. It's like I am watching, without involving in them.

Okay. So you're sitting here hearing the sound of water in the fishpond and you're observing yourself. Then you could ask, 'Who is hearing?' You can do that with everything that happens. 'Who is riding the bike? Who is sitting at the computer? Who is meeting a friend?'

Reminders to Stay Present

I think there would be no words at all if I continued asking myself these questions.

That would be wonderful, wouldn't it? Then you would come to the conclusion that nobody is eating lunch. Nobody is riding the bike. Nobody is meeting a friend. Because you would discover there isn't any 'I'. This nobody is consciousness.

If the 'I' disappears, then all the concepts also disappear.

All the concepts certainly disappear. What I'm suggesting is that you just decide you're going to investigate this 'I' all day long – at work and when you are communicating with people ask yourself, 'Who is talking now?' When you get angry ask, 'Who is angry?' Relentlessly, from early morning until late you're going to check this out for yourself. You're going to do it for you, and just see what happens.

Most of the time we are not present with what is actually happening but are preoccupied with movies and stories that are going on inside our head. Realising this creates an opening where we can begin to see that all of these stories come down to the more fundamental story of who 'I' really am, because this 'I' – my life, my story, me – is the crux of how it all works.

If you want peace and happiness in your life, if you want to become awakened, enlightened in this life, then you will inevitably be faced with this question of the 'I'. We believe in the false 'I'. We believe we are these beliefs and desires, this whole package we call 'my life'. It is this wrong identification with the idea of a separate 'I', a separate somebody, that is the barrier to our living in an awakened state – what this book is calling the Great Misunderstanding.

The Truth is we are already enlightened. We were always enlightened, and it is not affected by any *idea* of who we are. There's nothing more to get, but most of us have dust covering the diamond and it doesn't shine. We are also usually looking in the wrong direction, focusing our attention outside in the apparent world rather than on our actual experience.

> *A Buddhist phones the monastery and asks the monk, 'Can you come to do a blessing for my new house?'*
> *The monk replies, 'Sorry, I'm busy.'*
> *'What are you doing? Can I help?'*
> *'I'm doing nothing,' replied the monk. 'Doing nothing is a monk's core business and you can't help me with that.'*
> *So the next day the Buddhist phones again, 'Can you please come to my house for a blessing?'*
> *'Sorry,' said the monk, 'I'm busy.'*
> *'What are you doing?'*
> *'I'm doing nothing,' replied the monk.*
> *'But that was what you were doing yesterday!' said the Buddhist.*
> *'Correct,' replied the monk. 'I'm not finished yet!'*

Everything we do, think and feel can be understood to come from the source. We can understand that from the source comes the mind and from the mind comes the world. Look inside, away from the world, away from the people, away from the objects back into the source of everything. That source is our true nature.

Ramana Maharshi was largely responsible for introducing the ancient practice of Self-enquiry to the West in the middle of the twentieth century. Here is how he described it:

> *You have to ask yourself the question 'Who am I?' This investigation will lead in the end to the discovery of something within you, which is behind the mind. Solve that great problem and you will solve all other problems.*

It's a very clear statement, but most of us are always busy with our conditioned mind. Right now you might be remembering that you

Reminders to Stay Present

left the heater on at home and be wondering if by now the whole house is on fire. How can you sit here quietly if you're thinking about the house burning down?

There's always something to worry about, to keep us away from the present. We very easily go into the constantly thinking busy mind. It has become such a habit that we easily lose any balance with the more natural part of the mind.

There are two pre-requisites for Self-enquiry. The first is that you are able to look at yourself with some self-awareness. This means watching what is going on inside – being aware of your body sensations and emotions and seeing how the thoughts arise.

The other pre-requisite is a quiet mind. Both can be facilitated through a practice such as meditation or Yoga. If your mind is very busy and full of thoughts, then it is difficult to practise Self-enquiry. Out of a quiet mind, in a natural way, will come the question 'Who am I?' It is a fundamental question and you can't escape it.

A scholar asked the young Ramana Maharshi a question about Self-enquiry: *'What is the means for constantly holding onto the thought, Who am I? How to remember?'* He gave a very simple answer:

> *When other thoughts arise, one should not pursue them, but should inquire, 'To whom do they arise?' It does not matter how many thoughts arise. As each thought arises, one should inquire with diligence 'To whom has this thought arisen?' The answer that would emerge would be, 'To me.' Thereupon if one inquires 'Who am I?', the mind will go back to its source, and the thought that arose will become still. With repeated practice in this manner, the mind will develop a skill to stay in its source.*

I would suggest that in the beginning you make Self-enquiry a practice. Put aside some time each day and sit in a quiet place with your eyes closed. This immediately removes a lot of the world from your attention and you will be left with your thoughts and feelings, body sensations, the odd sound. Become aware of your thoughts

Rubbing out the Doodles

and then ask, 'To whom are these thoughts arising?' The answer will be 'To me.' Then you investigate the nature of 'me' by asking, 'Who is this me?' As the thoughts about 'me' settle down you will eventually drop into that quiet place inside.

'Who feels pain in the leg?' 'Me.' 'Who is me?' Just in this way. In the beginning it's a little bit like doing something, it requires some effort, but after a short time it will become very easy. It is important to ask both the questions, but you will find your own way of asking them. The beauty of it is that it switches your focus from the outside to the inside. Rather than identifying with the objects and experiences of the world, we become familiar with our true nature.

Self-enquiry is suggesting that your life is an opportunity to constantly come back to the source. As you bring Self-enquiry more into your life, the effect is like rubbing out the 'me' that you are so identified with. That may sound a bit scary, but don't worry about this. You've created something that you believe to be true, so you may rightly be afraid when it starts getting rubbed out. But the reality is, it never existed. Any words I might say about this don't make sense because there is no way for the mind to understand it. The understanding has to be from your own being, from deeper than the mind.

It's very difficult to really see that what you are so identified with could be false. Ramana Maharshi has so beautifully brought this ancient wisdom back to our attention. All you need to do is to get on with your life, and as you're going through your typical day you have those two questions running inside you.

Then, constantly, they will bring you back. Back to what? Stillness. Stillness. Stillness. Your body will still be alive. You will still be able to function, but you will not be caught up in your old identification. You will no longer believe yourself to be a somebody.

When you do find yourself totally lost in the clouds of thought and identification, try to remember to do Self-enquiry. When you do it, you merge with the Self. Your whole awareness is just there in this stillness. It's as if the world then disappears. We only know the world through our senses but when we come deeply into the Self we're not so busy with our senses and it's as if the world fades or becomes like a shadow. The clouds simply dissolve and you are back with the open sky.

> *A man goes to his front door to pick up his newspaper. He opens the door, bends down and notices that there is a small snail sitting peacefully next to the newspaper. The man picks up his newspaper and casually flicks the snail off into the bushes. Two years later there's a knock at the man's door. He opens it, and there's the same snail looking up at him with angry, red cheeks. He shouts up at the man 'Hey! What the hell was that all about?*

Self-enquiry reminds us to stay 'at home', to stay with our true Self. It constantly brings the mind back to its source. It is a one hundred and eighty degree turn from always focusing outside in the world to what's happening inside. You become an observer, a witness to what's going on inside. For example, if you focus on watching your thoughts you will see that one thought is followed by another and that you identifying them as 'my' thoughts. But they are only thoughts.

With Self-enquiry we are not interested in the subject of the thought. We are interested in the source of the thought. By continuously going to the source of the thought a kind of magic happens. You find that the thoughts get less and it becomes easier just to be quiet. You still have a mind, and if you need the mind to drive the car or to cook lunch then it is always ready.

Somebody who is truly free has a mind that, when it's not being used, is simply still or empty. It is receptive and responsive and when it is needed it activates itself, responding spontaneously to whatever is needed. It is fresh and innocent.

The King's Banquet
Self-Enquiry Opens Us to Freedom

The large room was completely still. Only a gentle breeze blowing through the windows and the sounds of the courtyard outside ruffled the stillness. I sat in a corner of the room, watching people on retreat sitting in pairs, facing each other and making soft and steady eye contact. This Satori Exercise was at the beginning of a day focusing on Self-enquiry.

I put on some soft background music and after some minutes I ask everybody to decide who is partner A and who is partner B. A will then ask B, 'Who are you?' while keeping eye contact. B says whatever he feels to say about this direct and penetrating question. Partner A doesn't engage in conversation at the response, but after some time again asks the question, 'Who are you?' This continues for some minutes.

The Satori Exercise naturally and beautifully reduces the answers to silence and presence. As time passes people often find it harder and harder to say anything in response to the question. After the time is up I ask everyone to close their eyes and just look to see if what they said about who they are is really true. The resulting silence is deep and heart felt. This is repeated with different partners for two to three hours, the whole room becoming quieter and quieter, moving towards stillness.

It's the first morning of the Summer Retreat, with an interesting mix of community residents and guests coming together for two weeks of silence and self-reflection. I find the Satori Exercise such a beautiful way to start a retreat because it is so incredibly effective in bringing us to peace, stillness and clarity. Yet we don't have to do anything. Peace is just waiting there under all the beliefs and ideas we have about ourselves. After the exercise I invited everyone to share, if they could, something about their experience.

•———•

There was an interesting sensation or feeling as if I was looking at myself from everywhere! I was looking at my thoughts, at my body sensations, at my emotions. There was no specific point in space from which I looked but it was like looking from all the space into myself. Without any judgment. Just a witnessing.

•———•

I feel quiet and vulnerable. During the exercise I could see a movement from the mind and emotions to this quiet and open space.

•———•

Each time I met a new person in the exercise I was aware of thoughts from my memory creating a picture of what is known. Each time the question came, 'Who are you?' it was like an unloading. Some thoughts started, they came into the space and then the question 'Who are you? and they were gone. It was very helpful for clearing the space.

•———•

Now is not different from what happened during the exercise – being present and receiving what comes in without being involved. There is not much going on; more like observing.

•———•

Something is melting. Slowly, slowly. It feels more warm, more quiet. It feels impossible to do or understand anything or to 'make' a shift. I can only wait for it – or not.

During the exercise there was the image that everything comes out of this silence, but to follow it brings me away from silence. Even trying to understand it brings me away from understanding.

There is a lot of energy, and so much sweetness in the heart. I could watch that it is completely enough just to be who I am, now, in this moment. I always tried to be different – but it doesn't work. It is enough to be what I am, now, just to accept that it is like this, now. That's all.

After lunch, in the shade of the walnut tree in the courtyard, a man who had been especially touched by the morning's exercise shared his experience.

As I was waiting for my turn to come out the front and speak I was preparing everything – what I would say, how I would behave. I do this quite often. Before it's my turn I get more and more nervous. This happens in all areas of my life, actually. I'm afraid that my life will pass and then suddenly, 'Ding! Okay! That's it! See you next time!' I'm so busy preparing how I will live that I don't actually live!

During the exercise I experienced a beautiful, empty space. It was actually very nice just to watch what I am not. I am not this beautiful music. I am not this beautiful feeling. Awareness is behind this; awareness is all these things. Because of this, everything becomes very beautiful.

Then I went back to my seat and was not so beautiful anymore. More and more I have the wish to enter this space, to receive this beauty, and yet it's passing. I miss it all because – because why? Because of what?

You map out the whole thing. It's lovely that you come, in the end of all that, to this fire inside. The fire wants to focus on the real thing.

Reminders to Stay Present

You should make it the first priority of your life. If it is the second priority, forget it. If you really want this beauty, this emptiness, then you have to be ready to give up everything the world appears to give you. If that's not possible, then forget it, because the rest of it is just a game. If you really want to be free, if you really want to merge with the emptiness, if you want to embrace this beauty, then you need one hundred percent focus. It only works if it's one hundred percent.

●——●

During the Satori Exercise a young woman who had been coming often to Satsang, suddenly, without any particular reason, started laughing uncontrollably. When the laughter subsided it was quite clear that something had shifted. Her face was very different and she was absolutely silent for the rest of the retreat.

The laughter was a signal that she had just seen the absurdity of what we call 'my life'. I would say that for at least a year she had been very close and it was only a matter of time. She was very interested and focused on that; it was her greatest priority. Then suddenly during the Satori Exercise it happened, just like that. You can say in that moment she knew it and in that knowing all the attachments to all the structures and stories just collapsed.

> *Two caterpillars are talking on a leaf when they see a butterfly flutter past. One caterpillar says to the other: 'You'll never get me up in one of those things!'*

Our nature is really like a butterfly but we seem to think we're caterpillars because all around us there are so many caterpillars. We are in the habit of being caterpillars but something doesn't feel comfortable because deep inside we know we are butterflies.

Becoming a butterfly can bring up a lot of fear for the little caterpillar. When you have this passion inside you, you move towards the edge. You don't think so much about what will happen.

The King's Banquet

You know that you want this and you go for it. Then suddenly, 'Oh, wait a minute! The lake might be full of crocodiles!' You don't know. Those rocks look pretty dangerous down there.

When you're close to the metamorphosis, 'you', the false you, senses the possibility that it could die. It becomes afraid. It could disappear, like a block of ice thrown into water. You suddenly realise this could actually happen and on one hand you absolutely want to take the leap, but on the other hand you question if you really want it because there's no coming back. I have experienced people becoming terrified because it seems exactly like death is approaching.

Over the last few years I have met many people who have glimpsed the beauty of 'butterfly'. Perhaps for five minutes, one minute, a few days, half a day, and there's no question they would ever want to come back. You can be thinking of buying a ticket on the ferry, but when you get there and realise the river is wide and it is only a one-way trip, then doubt and fear can arise. The metamorphosis has to come from a deep longing, a fire inside.

To help ground this sensation of being home, of being 'butterfly', one of the most powerful devices I can encourage is just to stay quietly alone. We are very used to relating all the time with a whole bunch of people in various situations and just to be alone is an amazing support, and interestingly it is very confronting.

The Island is a weekend retreat I offer that supports the practice of staying quietly alone. Each person has their own island – a mattress, a chair, a cushion and a blindfold. You stay on your island blindfolded for the whole weekend. There are assistants to make sure everyone is alright and to take you to the bathroom and bring food and drinks. It is such a powerful exercise for looking inward because nothing is happening on the outside. There is no relating going on with the world or with anybody. The room is in silence.

Two days is not so long, but several times during the weekend one or two people in a group of twenty have had very strong reactions, including vomiting and emotional pain. One man had driven a truck into a crossing when his brakes failed and had killed someone. It was an accident from years before but in the quiet space of The

Reminders to Stay Present

Island he couldn't deal with the pain that arose and had to leave. So being quiet can put us in touch with long-buried traumas. Nothing was happening externally to trigger an emotional drama. They were simply sitting alone on their island and something happened inside so strong that the body started to respond.

As a variation on The Island I've introduced a Retreat Cellar, which is a cave-like room, half underground. We've created a very earthy and womb-like feeling. Food is delivered through a slot in the door and you can stay there in complete isolation for a week or more.

People who come to The Island or stay in the Retreat Cellar often share that in the beginning the mind is extremely busy – even more busy than usual – but as they stay longer alone it eventually gives up and there are long periods of silence. After taking off the blindfold everything is experienced in a more intense way, and many people share that they don't want to meet or talk to anyone. They feel very, very good alone.

When you really stay alone you see that you don't need to reach out to someone who you hope will give you something. What you experience, just on your own, is an enormous sense of wellbeing, nourishment and love.

Once upon a time there was a king who wanted to give away his whole kingdom. He organised a wonderful party just for this. There was so much delicious food, lots of Swiss chocolate and wine and beer. There were people to entertain with wonderful music and dance and magic shows. The whole kingdom was invited.

The day of the party arrived and the king was waiting to be approached by anyone who was interested in being given his whole kingdom.

Everyone came to the party and enjoyed the food, the drink, the singing and the dancing and soon forgot about the king. He called his prime minister and asked what had happened because he was waiting to give away his kingdom and he had been sitting alone the whole evening. The prime minister explained that everyone was simply happy with the food, the drink and the entertainment.

There's always one more party, there's always one more person to meet, there's always one more story to hear. There's always something. The world is absolutely abundant. It has been set up like that. We always want to go out there; we always want to go into a story.

As you discover in the Satori Exercise, the Retreat Cellar or at home with yourself, you feel fantastically good, even though apparently nothing is happening. You just feel good for no reason. The whole kingdom is on offer. Don't get caught up with the feast and the entertainment. The kingdom is not far away. It's very close because this kingdom, in fact, is you. You're not separate from that. You *are* the kingdom.

Be Quiet
Leaving the Stories and Coming to Peace

After a meeting in Leipzig earlier this year we went to a Chinese restaurant for dinner. One of the people in the group was a professor of Indian studies. She was about fifty, and twenty years before she had been very interested in enlightenment. She decided to become a professor of Indian studies so that she could really come deeply into this search for enlightenment. She studied Sanskrit so she could read the ancient texts and she visited India several times. Now she told me very sadly that after twenty years she had never met stillness or peace. I said it was no problem and that if she could make a little time tomorrow morning I could show it to her very easily.

She said, 'Well, you know, I'm very busy. I'm a professor and I have a lot of appointments.'

I said, 'Come on. This is your life's desire. I'm not joking around with you; come tomorrow morning and I can almost certainly show you this.'

She cancelled her appointments and came to meet me. I offered her a Guided Self-enquiry. We sat together in an almost empty room and for twenty minutes I guided her away from her mind, away from her professor drama to stillness. I asked her to observe what was happening inside and to accept whatever that was. It took hardly any time at all and she was really touched. She just sat there, absolutely quiet, tears running down her cheeks.

Suddenly her mobile phone rang. Immediately she said, 'Oh, I'm really sorry that my phone has rung.' I didn't care at all because what does it matter? Let the telephone ring. Ringing telephone, not ringing telephone, it doesn't make any difference to stillness. As soon as she spoke, her mind started again and she lost touch with the stillness. Her mind again became busy as she was caught up in 'it's not okay as it is'.

If you have some moments of stillness you can say, 'Okay, I have "my life" and I have a few moments of stillness. These moments are an experience of my true nature.' Or you could say, 'I have my true nature, but most of the time I have an experience of "my life".' Just be with the quiet moments and see that all the rest, everything you call 'my life', is an experience. It's not you. When this understanding becomes really clear then it is possible to live in that stillness most of the time.

I asked the professor to stay for a short while so we could share about the stillness she had experienced.

It was so beautiful, but now I feel that I cannot get it back. As my day-to-day life starts up again I feel the pressure building inside as I think about not being in touch with this.

Well, it's very funny and very simple. You just sat on a chair and closed your eyes. Twenty minutes later you were having the most beautiful moment of your life, and you didn't do anything, did you?

That's right. I know that I get very busy and that I will go straight into it as soon as I get back to work or even get back home.

Just sit with your eyes closed and look inside. You can do it at home or even at work. Sit down, close your eyes and look inside in a very relaxed way. Don't try to change anything. If your mind is full of thoughts, let it be full of thoughts. Accept whatever is going on and you will sink down much deeper than your mind. If it doesn't work, you have to come here to another meeting! That's all that you have to do, so it's not really any kind of doing.

Reminders to Stay Present

The Guided Self-enquiry that I made with the professor is something I often do with my students to help them come through the mind to the vast emptiness inside. There is guidance and encouragement to say what is happening and simply accept whatever is there. Usually there are strong thoughts or emotions, but by continually accepting, without any judgment, something else is seen, something underneath the noise and activity of the mind and emotions.

One of my students asked me about this exercise. He visits occasionally and had seen it done before but had never been able to connect to what was being offered. He was direct and clear that he wanted to experience what he knew was there, underneath his thoughts and feelings.

Close your eyes and sit comfortably. Just look inside and see what is going on; be aware of whatever is there. Probably some thoughts, maybe some feelings, body sensations, or it might be quiet. Bring your attention to whatever seems to be the strongest and stay with that. Don't try to change anything. You don't have to do anything, you just observe. Now tell me what you find.

There is nothing stronger there, but the mind creates something stronger. Beyond this creation of the mind it's like 'is-ness' or 'space-ness'.

Okay. Stay with whichever of those seems to be strongest – just bring your attention there. (Silence) What's happening now?

There are some sensations in the body that seem to bring tension.

Just stay with that sensation in the body. (Silence) And now?

There is heaviness, heaviness of the moment.

Stay with what you are calling 'heaviness of the moment'. (Silence)

And now?

There is nothing there, but the mind creates something. There is a stream of thoughts.

Stay with the thoughts. You don't have to do anything; you don't have to change anything. Just be with what is. (Silence) And now?

Nothing there. Nothingness.

Just stay with this nothingness. (Silence) What's happening now?

It has always been there. (Silence)

What's happening now?

(He tries to speak, but then starts breathing heavily. Something strong is happening to him. Long silence)

It feels so good.

When you are ready, open your eyes. There you are, you're fifteen minutes away from what never changes.
 Even with open eyes it's there. It could be still there when you move around. It's so close and so easy. The fastest way to come to what never changes is just to be quiet and accept what is. Unfortunately, we've been conditioned to always look for a better deal.
 We don't need anything. This is the Truth that we can't talk about and we can't really understand. I could ask him but he couldn't really explain what's going on right now because nothing is going on; it's a strange paradox. We have such a strong idea that we need to get something in order to be happy, but this idea is exactly the reason why we're never happy. Really hear this. The reason we're never happy is because we believe we need something to make us happy.
 We try to make the world exactly as we would like it to be; we try

to control every moment because we have the idea that if the world could be perfect we could be perfectly happy. Unfortunately the world is quite complicated and we can never really get it. What we can do is to accept it exactly as it is, and then there would be absolutely no suffering. In fact, there would just be peace. One way of defining peace is to be without desire. No desire means not changing anything; it means just accepting everything as it is, even if you don't like it. The one who likes and the one who doesn't like – which we are completely identified with – is just an illusion.

Can you describe it? Is it a big space inside?

Yes, but somehow it doesn't matter. I don't know what to say.

Actually you can't really speak. Any words sound ridiculous. Inside you are drowning in silence.

Thank you!

Yes, I did all that! It's very important to realise that I had nothing to do with it. You can go away now from this meeting and find somewhere to sit quietly and just do the same thing. Just look inside.

We have so many ideas, but if you sit quietly and look inside you come quickly to that which doesn't change. You don't come to this place if you fight everything that you find. If you read a book that says you should have an empty mind then every time there's a thought you say, 'Oh! I shouldn't have this thought,' that creates tension. But if you simply look and accept whatever you find then those thoughts disappear. Feelings and body sensations also disappear. Then you are left with nothing, and that nothing is always there. It's very simple. Incredibly simple. It's just what is.

Now you have the map and you know how to get there. Maybe the map varies slightly each time, but it always starts with 'something' and ends up with 'nothing'. It's there for everybody, always.

Being quiet has the power to bring you to your true nature where you feel very nourished, very good. There's no feeling to go to any other place. We call this peace. Being quiet is a signpost pointing you to your true nature, which is always present, but we lose touch with it because we get preoccupied with the conditioned mind and all the exciting movies being offered.

When you close your eyes and become quiet you will gradually begin to notice some gaps between the thoughts. If you bring your attention to those gaps the thoughts begin to disappear and the gaps expand. Eventually, the gap is all there is. There may still be some thoughts, but they are far away. In the immediate awareness is a kind of nurturing emptiness. Nothing is happening, but you feel very good.

There is no sense of wanting to go anywhere. There is no desire. There is a deep contentment. You feel at home. You become aware of tremendous love that seems to reach out to include everything. You feel absolutely one with everything. In that moment all words become impossible. You experience a deep ecstasy and the response of the body to this ecstasy can be tears of overwhelming joy.

This is not happiness. It is a completely different dimension. It is peace, authentic love, pure awareness. This ecstasy is our true nature, and there is no one to know that. It just is.

There aren't really any words that can describe this. It is beyond words. It is where the words come from. It is the source of the words, the source of the mind and the source of the world. You are not separate from That. You *are* That. You will not understand it with your mind, but you will always know it.

If you become quiet then inevitably your true nature will be revealed. When you are not quiet, when the mind is active, you identify with your thoughts and dramas and can't come into contact with your true nature. You always keep yourself busy with some story so as not to meet the emptiness.

> *Jake, a passionate golfer, contacts a spiritual medium and asks, if there is a golf course in Heaven. The medium tells him that this is a strange request, but she will try to find out*

and get back to him in a few days. After several days, Jake gets a call from the medium.
'What did you find out?' Jake asks.
'Well, I've got good news and bad news for you,' says the medium.
'Okay, what's the good news?'
'That there is a beautiful thirty-six hole golf course in Heaven, and you'll have twenty-four-hour access with your own personal caddy,' answers the medium.
'And the bad news?'
'You're due to play at 9:30 on Sunday morning!'

All this enormous effort to do something causes us so much pain and suffering. When you are not 'doing' your life you can enjoy the possibility of life unfolding in the most unexpected way from moment to moment. You can live in this mystery. It's never possible to know what will come in the next moment. Surrender. Just be present and accept what is. Let it unfold and then simply respond. Actually, there is nothing really to do.

When you are absolutely still, when you are there as the Self, there is emptiness, nothing, a potential that responds from moment to moment without the baggage of 'my life'. When you are just quiet, then everything unfolds in the moment and the most simple things can touch you deeply. You are available for the beauty and lightness of life but the interesting thing is that you just know, and it is a knowing deeper than the mind.

During every retreat, we do something I call the Original Face, a simple exercise of being present. It's an amazingly effective way to come in touch with our potential emptiness. The retreat participants come one by one to sit at the front facing all the others. For six minutes they make quiet eye contact with everyone. Each participant takes their turn and so this goes on for three to four hours. Just by focusing on the eyes and absorbing the still energy they become present.

Presence means that the organism is simply here, the Self is radiating and there is no conditioned mind. Sitting up in front of a group of open-hearted people during the Original Face and just being there, quiet and present, the activity of the mind is automatically cut away. After this simple act of making eye contact, one woman shared something very beautiful about her experience in that moment.

It's difficult to speak now, probably also to move or stand up. I felt I knew silence, and felt that there would be something after it, something grand and profound. Just looking around at the people there's no desire to move. Absolute contentment just to be here.

Yes. It doesn't mean that the body won't move, but inside there is a still point. Whatever you do, wherever you go, it's just still, and this person called 'me' doesn't exist anymore. Just emptiness. It is a moment when you experience existence in a completely new way — simply by being quiet – and you are just present.

When nothing is happening, nothing is happening. When something is happening, something is happening. There is no desire or intention, and you're completely content just with 'what is'. Without even noticing it, it's total surrender. That's what surrender means: acceptance of what is. When you are able to welcome that into your life, or rather ground your life in that, it is the most wonderful way to live. It's really simple!

Oh yes! It's like eating the best honey. Inside there is a very deep feeling that I have come home.

Existence gives us this amazing paradise. You only have to go outside and walk along the river, with the sun shining and the breeze blowing. It's completely beautiful, even in the middle of winter. Everything is amazing! The sky, the clouds, the vast space, the flow of water in the vast river. But we can't even be here for this beauty because as we walk along the river, what happens? We remember something that somebody said to us yesterday, '… and I got so upset and he didn't understand me …'

The possibility – amazingly – is not what you really expect. You're probably expecting all kinds of amazing practices, theories, principles and philosophies, but what is real can best be discovered by being quiet. The more you can be quiet the more likely you are to come to this beauty inside. It is the same beauty for everybody. It's one beauty, one peace, and it never changes. Tremendous peace, oneness, and inner nourishment. That's our nature; that's our Truth.

It is only possible to come to your true nature when you don't *do* anything at all. Then the Self radiates and everything that manifests is manifesting from the Self. Just be quiet and there you are. There you always are.

The Importance of 'Thank You'
Life is a Mirror

Today some of the residents are rushing around the house carrying boxes full of their clothes and shelves full of books. There is a two-week fair in town and many guests will be coming to the area, so our guesthouse needs as many free rooms as possible. In this situation some people move from their rooms, taking everything with them, and stay in the dormitory. The extra money helps residents buy their yearly tickets to the Indian retreat.

People were just starting to get a little settled as only two months before all the sleeping spaces had been rearranged. It is an intense time, because on top of all the other projects and tasks to keep the community running, some residents are rushing around, uprooting themselves from their comfortable rooms.

Living in society, it's completely normal and common to behave and think as we've been conditioned to. When we refer to 'me' we are referring to this conditioned package – my life, my story. One of the points of the work here in the community is to examine all of that and to try to get some distance to see the extent of it. Being able to honestly observe ourselves and to see how much our particular situation has conditioned us is not easy.

A natural consequence of living closely together is that our comfort zone often gets a good shake, and a big part of my function is to keep the shaking up going. Even something as simple as moving rooms and having to shift belongings can really shake us because most of us have the expectation that we need our own room. But funnily enough, when you come to live in a community it's not very important anymore. In fact, people positively enjoy sharing space. The flow of community life puts much less emphasis on 'mine', and so there is much more sharing of anything we call personal.

All our days are full of activity and in this kind of intensity there are so many mirrors for people to see facets of themselves. Through working so closely together, everybody exposes themselves. All our structures and patterns become clear to the others, who act as mirrors to reflect them back to us. This is actually quite a rare situation. It's not something which is readily available, and unless you live with people who understand and support this process then it's much more difficult to really focus on what goes on inside you. Mirrors are everywhere, not just in community, but you will need to be very focused and have a very strong intent to get the full benefit from them.

We have developed some devices to help us see our structures. One device we call the STOP! game. A person is chosen to run the game and when they call out STOP! everyone freezes. Then we take a few moments to become aware of what is running through our minds. We get to see what is operating in that moment and how much energy we are giving it. By stopping we can see it, and once it is exposed in this way it loses some of its power. This device was inspired by George Gurdjieff, who created a community he called The Institute for the Harmonious Development of Mankind, a beautiful possibility that inspires our community.

Another device we use is the Buddy System. Each person has a 'buddy' who they work very closely with through the day and who really gets to know them. When we see our buddy doing one of their favourite mind structures, we gently point it out to them. It's very important that the buddy then says 'thank you', because without a genuine sense of gratitude there is always the possibility that it can be received as just another judgment.

> *A family was having dinner on Mother's Day. For some reason the mother was unusually quiet. Finally the husband asked what was wrong. 'Nothing,' said the woman. Not buying it, he asked again. 'Seriously, what's wrong?' 'Do you really want to know? Well, I'll tell you. I have cooked and*

The Importance of 'Thank You'

cleaned and fed the kids for fifteen years and on Mother's Day you don't even tell me so much as "Thank you".' 'Why should I?' he said. 'Not once in fifteen years have I gotten a Father's Day gift.' 'Yes,' she said, 'but I'm their real mother.'

We all have a very strong, deep defense mechanism called denial, but anyone entering into the Buddy System is ready to go beyond denial to what is true. We say 'thank you' because we realise that by getting help to see our structures, we can gradually get free of them. As soon as we bring awareness to them, they have less hold on us. This understanding is implicit in our 'thank you'.

One of the founding residents recently took me aside to look at the difficulties she was having with me being one of her buddies.

———•———

Are you able to thank your buddy?

Yes. When my buddy tells me something maybe I try to defend myself with, 'Well, are you sure? Was it not different?' But I more or less give in immediately because actually I want to see what she has seen. I want to learn something about myself, so why should I fight? I asked her to be my buddy and I want to hear what she has to say. But with you it's a bit more difficult!

Yes, it's not so easy for you when it comes from me. Why do you think you have such a strong reaction to me but not to your everyday buddy?

She doesn't give me such a tough time. I have a different role with her and she has a different role with me, so she doesn't trigger it.

No, she doesn't. That's the point! It seems clear that for some time you have projected the pain you associate with your father's love onto me.

Reminders to Stay Present

Oh! It's so difficult.

The reality is it's difficult for most people, and it's only when you've worked through the easier stuff that you're ready for the more difficult questions. We have known for years that sooner or later you would have to deal with issues about your father. It is very strong for you and also probably has a lot of pain attached to it.

Yes, that's true.

I just become this horrible guy who's always putting you into pain. You have to come to a clear understanding about what's happening. Of course, I'm not interested in creating pain for you.

I believe you, so I always wonder how it happens. I don't believe you want to give me pain, but I feel it.

I can't give you pain. I don't have to give it to you because you've already got it. I'm just reminding you that you have all this pain inside. 'Thank you' is very important, otherwise you're going to project on to me that I'm your abusive father who did all those horrible things to you. We feel some pain and immediately we resist what is being said.

I even have the feeling it's completely reasonable that I feel resistance: 'That's really too much!!'

It's very important that if I'm going to trigger old memories you have to thank me for doing it. It is so valuable that somebody is doing that for you. It's not valuable if you just take it as a judgment.

It's not so easy.

That's why 'thank you' is so important. If you don't say it – and feel it – you will just react from your unconscious, robotic structures.

The Importance of 'Thank You'

You have to understand the opportunity. Without going into the psychology, you have to at least understand this mechanism.

Yes, I basically understand that.

Nobody is giving anybody pain. You have the pain and people can trigger it in certain situations. Everybody should really remember this 'thank you'. If you don't thank your buddy, even if in that moment you don't go into reaction, it's very possible that later something will start working and then you will avoid your buddy because the reminder can bring pain. In one way it's natural to want to avoid pain, but actually you have to stand in the pain to be free of it. 'Thank you' is to trick that mechanism.

———

Our community is actually just a microcosm of the world. We have the same experiences, but we have made it a priority to look at our reactions to these experiences as a way of finding out about ourselves.

It never helps to blame our difficulties on somebody else. If our priority is to find out who we are, we can use these difficulties as mirrors in which to see ourselves. Life itself is a mirror. We don't have to wait for special times or places before we look at ourselves. We can even just say 'thank you' quietly to every situation that triggers something in us – to the petrol station attendant who is being so slow, to your neighbour's son cranking up the music, and so on.

I would say the essence of a spiritual life is to know who you are, and you can find out who you are at any moment. I have known people who have woken up in a supermarket and in a laundromat. Everything that happens in life is an opportunity to know yourself. In our modern society most people are simply not interested to know who they really are.

The big structure we're trying to see is our identification with being a separate somebody: 'me'. By looking at our reactions over some time, by looking at ourselves, we can become aware of our different patterns.

Reminders to Stay Present

The real spiritual work when living with a teacher – which is happening on a deep level in our community – is that the teacher will take away your ego, your story. He will slowly, surgically, remove it, slice by slice, trying to keep it within the balance of pain. He doesn't want too many people dying on the operating table! He performs a most delicate type of brain surgery to take away all your favourite illusions.

Most importantly, the teacher is a mirror, and the closer you get, the stronger the mirror. This mirror brings all the things that we don't want to look at right up into our face. It's not wrong to have many issues. If you still believe 'that's me', then it's a pity, but they will be there! The more open your heart becomes the more these issues are there in your face. The teacher is the strongest and clearest buddy and that also makes him the most difficult to say thank you to.

This can be very uncomfortable, and in fact many teachers are more popular when they're dead than when they're alive because when they're dead they can't show you your issues! But what about all this stuff that you don't want to see? Unless you understand it and accept the things you don't want to see, you will never be free of them.

Over the last two years I have been working with a close student on her strong issues about arrogance. Living with a community of people it is not so easy to be arrogant and to get away with it all the time. For example, this student is famous for saying, 'I know!' We are all wrong and she is right. She knows.

This confident face usually covers up the exact opposite feeling that is really happening inside – that actually she doesn't know. The work begins in the community to show her this arrogance so that she can become free of something that doesn't serve who she really is.

It needs its time, however long that is, for this glass to break, and it is not an easy process to have something taken away that is very familiar and which gives a sense of security. It's such an interesting and amazing process that I invited the student to come and talk about it during Satsang.

The Importance of 'Thank You'

Would you like to share something about the destruction of the glass, the process you've been involved in for a couple of years now?

I don't really know what to say. It's very difficult to have the glass broken, to let go of something strong inside, or even just to see it!

I remember you being very sure about yourself. You gave a sense of being rather confident about who you are. It didn't feel very real to me. What you are describing now is closer to the truth than what you were describing two years ago.

Through this process I come more and more to the emptiness, and that feels more and more vulnerable. Still, I feel that I do not see the reality of who I am. If I am not this false self, what is the reality?

The reality is that you are an entity. You have a mind, you have a body, and it all functions very naturally. The invitation of life is to respond to every moment, but human beings have developed this false self and this takes precedence over the pool of emptiness. We have so much confidence in the character we have created and the role we have adopted that we don't question them.

At least you're not so sure of the reality of your role anymore. Your sense of who you are and your sense of the world are being shaken. You are bound to feel vulnerable because suddenly you don't have this nice feeling of 'my' character, of who 'I' am. Things that made sense last week don't really make sense anymore. Things that seemed to be solid suddenly start to move. Yet this vulnerability is a beautiful opportunity because if you continue to be available you will discover the Truth of who you are.

We have ideas that who we are will be something very special, very wonderful, very out of the ordinary – something called 'enlightenment'. As we fall into this mystery we discover something that's actually very simple – in the Truth of our being there is a space that we can call 'emptiness'. This space is not as we might imagine emptiness to be because it contains everything. Along the way we discover that this emptiness is the essence of life. This is a remarkable discovery, and it is absolutely available – to everyone. No special requirements are needed, only an availability. Can you see the benefit of that glass breaking?

Yes, completely.

However you still resist the breaking?

Yes, because it's such a habit to hold on to my old ways of behaving, particularly ones I don't even know about.

From the bigger picture you can see all the benefits, but still there is resistance to breaking the next piece of glass.

Each time something comes up where another piece of glass could break, I get very scared – because I know it will be painful.

It's a bit like having a plaster on your hairy leg. You can take it off very slowly and not have much pain or you can pull it off quickly, experience the pain, and then it's over. It happens in different ways for different people.

Probably you hated your mother in the moment when she did that, but at the same time you understood it was necessary and you loved her anyway, even if it hurt. Try to see me as a very loving nurse taking your old plasters off your hairy legs!

I do this regularly to my young daughter. She cries because it's very painful but later on she thanks me.

It is hard to explain, but the more the mother – or in this case the teacher – hurts you, the more they love you. If you don't love somebody you don't care enough to remove the plaster when it needs to come off. The spiritual teacher loves you and wants to support you to become free. He understands that sometimes he has to pull the plasters off. Can you then say thank you?

After some hours or days! Thank you.

The reason the world is not full of enlightened people is that almost everybody runs away when they come to their pain threshold, to this sheet of strong glass. As far as I can see, the reason why people don't become really free is because they don't keep going until the end.

To become free it is important to have someone who can really see your story and reflect it back to you. It's only this illusion that you've created that prevents you from awakening. The whole effort of the teacher is to create some mechanism for you to see that, and once you do, it's all finished.

The effect of this intense mirroring – from people, from the teacher, from life itself – is to come to a moment when you realise without any doubt that you're not who you've always imagined yourself to be. This is a very beautiful and life-changing moment because now you see the possibility of living *not* from the conditioned mind.

The whole focus of our community and all the retreats and weekends is to create an environment where this is more likely to happen. We use the games and exercises to help us become more aware, but the whole of life is a beautiful invitation and an opportunity to see yourself – wherever you are and whatever you are doing in the world.

Chapter 7
Awake and Free

Nothing is missing!
What is really true is just now!
We have this moment;
that's all.
With this understanding
life becomes paradise –
because you are truly free.
Free from everything you call 'me'.
The way to live an awakened life
is to simply be.

Chapter 7
Awake and Free

In this space of stillness, you may come to a moment when the old perception of the world and yourself drops away and you have a deep insight into your true nature. If this glimpse becomes grounded in you, you can live constantly from your true nature. What will you do when daily life doesn't bother you anymore? Will you still be able to function? Life can be enjoyed as it is in every moment, expressing itself naturally through you in joyful creativity, peace and constant celebration of the moment.

Celebration and Natural Creativity ... 207
Celebrate Now

Soap in the Mercedes ... 213
The Mystery of Life

The Glimpse ... 219
Awakening From the Illusion

Tales of Awakening ... 227
Sharing Moments of Liberation

Living in Freedom ... 240
Paradise Now

Celebration and Natural Creativity
Celebrate Now

I don't make much of birthdays, especially my own, but this year was an exception as I felt it would be a good chance for the whole community to come together for an evening of celebration. It was not to celebrate the day I was born; rather the birthday was just a good excuse to celebrate for the sake of celebrating. We decided that after a delicious dinner everyone would present a small performance, something creative that came uniquely from each person.

While this plan was received with mixed interest from the residents, the result was a great variety of performances. There was a drumming piece, a song, some theatre and even a lap dance! Each expression was unique and beautiful, and in some cases it was really quite a challenge for people to express themselves in such an open and authentic way.

It is challenging because you have to be yourself. You can't really put on a mask when you are expressing something dear to you or close to your heart. For some, it is difficult to expose themselves in this way.

It was such a great evening because there was no point to it. There was endless creativity and a lot of laughter, but there was no real plan, just spontaneity. Expressing oneself authentically is a huge step on the path to awakening, and ultimately results in something very simple but very beautiful – living each moment in innocence and presence.

Over the last eight years in the community the energy of creativity has grown. More and more we have energy for theatre, dance, music, sculpting, painting. It is something very natural. In the beginning I might have thought, 'Well, I'm a painter, I'm a

Awake and Free

creative kind of person, so maybe the people who have come to me are also creative people.' But I dont think that's particularly the case. I think that as we find ourselves becoming quiet, we find ourselves becoming more creative.

As you come into silence and emptiness, as your mind has less and less of a hold on you, what is there to do? We are here and we have a life, so what to do with this life? Without really choosing anything, creativity naturally comes out of the silence. The more you are 'not there' the stronger the flow of creativity.

I'm sure you have experienced this yourself. Perhaps you have been dancing, singing, painting or even gardening and at a certain moment the 'somebody' who is doing it disappears. You are totally absorbed in the activity and you forget that 'you' are doing it. When that happens you feel a tremendous ecstasy inside and actually this has nothing to do with the activity itself.

One of our residents is notorious for being shy and embarassed by displays of self-expression, so the worst thing happened to him when he was invited onto the stage to join in a theatre sketch. He was immediately locked into his mind – into his self-doubt and insecurities – and out of his heart, out of his natural being.

While the party dispersed I sat with him over the last of the evening's champagne, talking about what had happened for him a couple of hours before.

I wanted to join in the performance on some level, but stepping up I felt an energy block. Performance is not something I am familiar with and so I felt a huge fear. My mind completely froze up. I also found it hard to breathe.

This feeling you describe is very common. An example I am familiar with is when you start to paint on a white paper. It's rather easy in the beginning: there's a lot of white and a little bit of colour. But as you put more and more colour in, it actually gets more difficult and then you can feel some resistance. You don't know what to do; you don't know where to put the colour. You don't know which colour to use. You don't know which side to brush. Suddenly, it gets very difficult. You have thoughts such as, 'I can't do this! I'm not good enough.' Looking at your neighbour's painting you think, 'Oh! My painting is not as good as his!'

You start just with a painting, or in your case with theatre, and very soon you're faced with all your structures, the false you.

But it feels so real, and I feel such a pressure to do something to come out of it. Is there anything to do, actually?

The structures you are coming up against are all the garbage that you have collected through your life. You can't really play! You feel shy, 'And anyway, he's such a good actor and I was never really any good!'

I suggested focusing on creativity this evening as a way of provoking these structures to appear. Without you doing anything, just the thought of being in that situation brings up so much. In the end, you can just watch what happens inside.

So if I continue with all this creative stuff, expressing and exploring myself, I will see more and more of my structures. Can I slowly become free of them just by seeing them?

Focus on a higher creativity. Create yourself into a Buddha. This is very, very beautiful, and it is like climbing to the summit of Mount Everest. This is the peak of human possibility in creativity.

It is possible. It is not possible to fly, but you *can* create a statue, a dance or a painting, and you can also create yourself into a Buddha. But it is a big job. You have to be really focused. It is not enough to go to three Satsang meetings, read two books and say hello to three or four teachers. It will require every drop of blood and every bit of energy in your body. But it is possible, and the whole flow of consciousness is inviting that.

The invitation is not to apply all your focus to paying your phone bill every month. The invitation is to create yourself into a Buddha and live at the highest peak of creativity and consciousness.

So now I focus my creativity onto creating myself into a Buddha!

On the absolute level, you are already a Buddha! Creating yourself into a Buddha actually means you just have to get out of the way, step aside and discover that you are already a Buddha. And then one Buddha expresses through painting and another through sweeping the courtyard, cooking lunch or playing music. It doesn't matter; the actual expression isn't very important.

I like my little joke that everybody arrives on this planet with an invitation around their neck saying something like 'welcome – have fun', but unfortunately it seems to fall off in many cases. We forget it very quickly, but probably part of us longs to come back to this natural playfulness that was there as a child. This is particularly true of people who have some kind of creative talent.

Within us we have a joyful, spontaneous, natural part and we also have a part that is conditioned and serious. When we come back to our true nature the natural part shines and life becomes joyful, spontaneous and playful. When you become very quiet, when this attachment to the false self is cut, there is something that wants to express from the stillness. It is as if the fundamental nature of consciousness wants to express itself.

Then you can just do your dance, and somehow we all find our own dance. If you don't feel any strong or clear expression in your life, then maybe you are already expressing something just by being here. The funny thing about existence is that all the different animals, birds, insects and human beings are constantly expressing something. It can't really be escaped. It is nothing personal but what is expressing is exactly you. It is consciousness manifesting through your particular mind-body entity. The whole of existence is pulsating

Celebration & Natural Creativity

and celebrating, without any reason.

We don't need a reason to enjoy and celebrate every moment. It is already enough to be breathing, to be hearing, to be seeing, to be expressing – that's already enough to celebrate. There doesn't need to be anything special. You don't have to be Picasso or Mozart. You can just paint or play the flute because you enjoy it. That's enough. Osho used to encourage celebration in each moment and conducted four huge special celebrations each year. Finally he proposed leaving up the coloured lights all year round saying, 'Every day you can celebrate your birthday!'

Our minds would love there to be some great master plan where we are all working towards some incredible perfection in the future. And what about now? It's very imperfect. One lot of people over here are busy cutting down all the beautiful trees and making them into little woodchips. And over there they are killing all the whales and making cat food. Lovely! At the same time another lot are busy planting trees and that lot over there are saving the whales.

So what's it all about? Maybe it isn't about anything. Maybe there's no point. Maybe the only point is to see that there is no point; that there is no future – there is only 'now'. Then what to do with this 'now'? Shall we postpone it to the future? 'Anyway, I'm very busy now. I need to go to the Internet cafe. How can I possibly be here now?' What if there's only this moment and nothing else? Then why not celebrate this moment? Why not take it and accept it and just be here for it?

> *A new monk arrives at the monastery. He is assigned to help the other monks in copying the old texts by hand. Pretty early on, he sees they are copying from copies, so he points out that if there were an error in the first copy, that error would be continued in all of the other copies.*
> *The head monk says, 'We have been copying from the copies for centuries, but you make a good point, my son.' So, he goes down into the cellar with one of the copies to check it against the original.*

> *Hours later, nobody has seen him. So one of the monks goes downstairs to look for him. He hears great sobbing coming from the back of the cellar and finds the old monk leaning over one of the original books and crying. He asks what's wrong. The old monk looks up with red eyes filled with tears and sobs, 'The word is "celebrate".'*

Just be, without any point. In India they have a wonderful word for this – leela. It means divine play. This is beautifully illustrated by children playing on the beach. They have a wonderful time building sandcastles. They are totally there for every moment as they build them up. They have a few disagreements together, but they absolutely enjoy the play of it. And then, of course, the afternoon at the beach comes to an end and Mummy calls out, 'We have to go now!' Then they have an equally wonderful time breaking down the sandcastles, jumping up and down on them. When you understand that there is only now, then you are enjoying the leela of life.

We would like there to be a very serious point, and we could say that the serious point is to know who we are. Then what do we do when we know who we are? Well, then we celebrate! It's almost the same: you know who you are, then you celebrate the moment, or you celebrate the moment and then, of course, you know who you are.

Soap in the Mercedes
The Mystery of Life

After returning home from a Satsang tour, I woke the next morning to find that in the night a student had filled up my petrol tank with soap powder. He had been upset by something I had said, and had been projecting strong feelings against me for some time. He had decided to leave in the middle of the night with his girlfriend, and had filled my tank with soap powder as he was leaving.

We asked the garage what we should do about the soap. They said 'Oh, just drive it until the tank is empty then change the filter and put in new petrol.' It was a Mercedes garage telling us this, so we believed them. We drove it and pretty soon the petrol pump stopped working, so we put in a new pump. It seemed to be okay, but then it stopped working again.

Back to the garage where they told us we needed a new exhaust system. Then the car seemed to be okay for a while but again it stopped working and the petrol pump was making a funny noise. So they put in a new pump for free but again it didn't work. After that we replaced the new petrol pump, put in a new petrol tank, replaced various pipes, pumps and filters and it *still* didn't work. Then it was another five hundred euros for some kind of pressure regulator and two days later they told us we needed two little sensors! Then they said 'Well, even then we're not sure it will work!'

Life happens the way it happens and not always in the way we would like it. I was not particularly happy about this situation with the car, but in the end I can say it was just like that. I'm alright and if the car is not alright, no problem! Me being alright is not dependent on the car being alright.

There is no possible way we could not be okay. We are absolutely perfect and there is no way we could be any different. We are always in exactly the right place and it is absolutely as it should be!

> *A disciple is on one side of a raging river. There are no bridges. He has no boat. He shouts out to the master on the opposite bank. 'How do I get to the other side?'*
> *The master shouts back: 'You are on the other side.'*

You're always in the only place you can be, and you can never know what's going to happen. Just choose to live the mystery. Maybe when I went to pick up the Mercedes after spending three or four thousand euros I would bend down and find a huge diamond wedged in the tyre! Maybe the last customer dropped the diamond out of her ring. Life is the most perfect roller coaster. We can never know.

Amazingly, the real diamond appeared only a few days after the upset student disappeared. The day after he left was an intensive weekend of Self-enquiry and a few days after the weekend we noticed that his wife, Kirsten, who lived in the community, was laughing a lot, apparently not experiencing any great tragedy at the disappearance of her husband with another woman. She was having a strong glimpse of her true nature.

Kirsten had gone shopping in the local village and as she was sitting outside the supermarket watching the people go by with their groceries she suddenly realised she wasn't in the film anymore. A great sense of freedom came from that, and I'm so happy for her. Her waking up was my diamond in the tyre and compensation for all the trouble with the car.

Before she came to the community, Kirsten was a regular housewife. She worked in a bank, looked after her child, and led a normal life. One day she decided to come with her husband to Satsang. After that her interest developed and she came to live in the community.

• ——— •

My husband and I wanted to live together in the community. He and our son came here right after the Summer Retreat, while I took care of packing up the house and finalising all our arrangements. Also I continued working for three days a week. Then he suddenly left and I don't think I ever laughed so much as on that weekend. It was really funny, like a story from a book of fairy tales. I could see that the past just doesn't exist anymore.

All your ideas about relationship, the world and 'my life' are just a fairy story that is playing in your mind, and now it has all been wiped clean. When you wake up you see that this big story, 'my life', is simply a fairy story and that it never really existed.

Can you tell us about the moment you had the strong opening?

We had just come out of the supermarket and we had a lot of shopping bags. It was quite a walk to the next shop, so I said, 'I'll just sit down on this bench and wait for you.' I watched people walking by and I noticed that it was like watching a movie in a cinema, and I was not in this movie. At some point the phone rang and I answered it. Someone asked me what they should cook for lunch. I told them, and the movie just went on. It is still going on and on and on, but there isn't anyone here.

Where do you think you lost the 'I'?

I have no idea.

Since you lost your 'I' you have driven to Nuremberg where you worked for a few days, arranged to send your furniture here, took care of your son, occasionally spoke to your ex-husband and laughed a lot.

Some people are very worried that if they would lose their 'I' they wouldn't be able to function anymore, but you seem to be functioning very well.

Even better than before.

How is that?

Before, I spent most of the time with thoughts about the future or the past or about what I have to do. Now, I'm just always in the moment. Right now I'm sitting here and telling this story and there are no other thoughts. All those other thoughts that had filled the mind before, they are just gone.

So everything is going along quite easily.

Yes, everything goes by itself.

By itself! Isn't this a wonderful way to live? Can you just imagine living in a flow, when there's no caring what's going to happen? Instead of retiring at sixty-five and getting your pension you can retire right now. Maybe there's no pension, but you can simply retire and let everything happen.

    Recently I have heard you say that all the feelings are welcome – sadness or joy or anything. Can you feel the different qualities?

It's actually all the same energy.

Sitting here in Satsang, you sometimes laugh a lot; when you're over there in the kitchen then you don't laugh so much. Do you feel stressed sometimes?

Of course there are some times when I'm stressed because there's a lot to do, but even then I'm laughing. When there is something funny I laugh, when there is not something funny then I don't laugh. This laughing is not something that I do – it just happens. If something funny happens then the laughter comes and when I'm doing some work I concentrate on whatever there is to do in that moment.

The fact that you can function better than before is very important because there is a real fear that if you would simply drop the whole story of 'my life', you would fall into a kind of grey nothing. But it's not like that.

I support myself by working three days a week in a bank where I function very well. Actually, even there it all works better than before. When I'm consulting with a customer I am just present in the moment with that person. I don't have any other thoughts and I still remember everything that has to be done.

Kirsten's glimpse continued and her self-awareness increased. She was an energetic member of the community while still working part time in the bank to support herself and her son.

The invitation, and that's the crux really, is to stay with the silent part and not get hooked into the movie. There is something that doesn't change, and to really get in touch with that you will find it helps to be quiet, not to be talking or activating the stories and the structures.

We are constantly making judgments about how our future should be. This is just part of our illusion, just part of doing 'my life'. But we can't know the future. When we have had a glimpse, when we are in touch with that which doesn't change, it is easy just to accept what is. We can't know the future. We're constantly making judgments – this is good, this is not good – but we can't really know it.

If you come to see this, then naturally something will relax. The invitation is to accept what is and drop the idea that 'I'm doing my life', that 'I know'. Then your life will have an easy flow. 'You' will dissolve away and daily life, which had many problems, will suddenly have a different texture. You will notice that things just seem to happen. They feel right, with no particular goal.

Life is seen as an unfolding from moment to moment. You become aware that you are identifying with something that never changes, that just is. It has the qualities of peacefulness and silence, a deep stillness, great wellbeing, the sense of being surrounded by a huge warm blanket, protected and nurtured. The world changes constantly. Our actions and experiences also change, but at our core there is something that never changes.

I'm reminded of the story about a young man who found a beautiful white horse. He brought it back to the village and everybody rushed out saying, 'Wow! You're so lucky; you've got this beautiful white horse!'

The next day he went riding. The horse threw him off and he broke his leg. When he came hobbling back to the village all the village people came out and said, 'Oh God! What a terrible horse! Look at what he's done to you – how horrible! Now you've got a broken leg!'

But the next day army recruiters came to the village looking for young men to take to the army, and naturally they couldn't take the young man with a broken leg. Then the villagers cried, 'Wow! You are so lucky! Because of the broken leg you can't go into the army.'

And of course, this story goes on and on. It's called life. While we watch our own movie, life continues. So-called problems are only judgments about some circumstance in life.

The Glimpse
Awakening from the Illusion

The house where the community is based is an extensive seventeenth century mansion with a maze of rooms spreading around a courtyard. We arrived in the summer of 2006, moving from a horse farm where we had started the community two years earlier. For the first few months, while not busy organising the moving process, we explored the old house. We found rooms behind rooms, closets behind closets, and many little spaces that could be used for interesting things. We found an enormous attic space hiding behind old boxes. We found an old stable with ancient riding equipment concealed behind some bushes, and we even found a wartime bomb shelter.

The best discovery was about three years later when someone was cutting wood in a corner of the courtyard and stumbled upon a small hatch concealed in the cobblestones. It led to a storage space of some kind, but it looked a lot like a cell in an old monastery. It was a beautiful surprise for those living here, and we turned it into a retreat cellar where you can be alone for some days. It is a beautiful little space, but one that no one knew existed for three whole years. How many times we walked over it or chatted near it or scuffed our shoes on its surface.

Making a discovery like this is a lot like discovering something about yourself that you had never seen before. Something that was always there, beneath all the things that cover it, something that is quiet and not strikingly obvious until you clear the old wood pile away and find the hatch. You find stillness, silence and peace that you never knew existed. When this happens in the sense of spiritual discovery, I call it a 'glimpse', a glimpse of your true nature, the underlying silence and stillness. Also it is a glimpse of a new possibility of how you can live your life.

A woman recently came as a volunteer to the house, choosing to live and work with us for some weeks. She joined an intensive weekend retreat, with mornings and evenings full of Satsang, stillness and enquiry. She was strongly affected, and after the weekend she had an intense glimpse of her true nature. She felt a great energy in her body and a sense of deep connectedness and bliss that she had never believed possible. She had seen who she was on a profound level.

However, the glimpse was temporary and she came back into what she knew, leaving her between worlds. She wanted to find out how to uncover all the hidden rooms inside herself, all the hidden possibilities, but she didn't know where to start. One evening I was talking about the potential of living in a state beyond the mind, beyond what we know, using the example of this woman's glimpse to show how close it is. She responded to this by coming up to share how she felt after her experience.

I seem to be in a situation where I cannot live the way you describe yet I cannot live any longer in the old way either. There is just effort and pain and I feel stuck.

So just after the retreat weekend you had a strong glimpse?

Yes, very much. My experience was an energetic opening in which I knew who I was; but then, almost immediately, something closed by itself and I was back in confusion.

This kind of sudden energetic opening is not Self-realisation because it is not permanent; the attachment to the false self is not permanently dissolved. But it was enough of an opening for you to have a glimpse of who you are. Now it's closed and you're back in confusion again.

If I look at you right now I can see that something is different from before. The intensive weekend was a total bombardment of all your false notions about life. It was like all-out war, and the effect of this is that everything has started to open up.

Yes, that's wonderful, because I came with the idea that I would have to 'do' something in order to get something.

We often come with an idea that we have to understand or learn something. Of course, those things happen, but more happens – things we don't even imagine. When we continue to make ourselves available to this bombardment, everything is blown apart. Our sense of our self is shaken and we can feel quite vulnerable, but by remaining available we will discover the Truth of who we are.

Yes! It completely changed me. All feeling that I had to do something, all of the old stories vanished, but only for two days. Then everything was worse than ever.

Once you drink champagne it's hard to drink cheap wine again. What's going on now is very positive. Before, you thought you knew who you were, and now you know that you don't know.

That is actually quite an important step. Most people believe they know who they are, and as a result everything feels quite comfortable and safe and solid. But as in your case, experiencing something much truer about yourself can make you feel very vulnerable and shaky and unsure about who you are. From my point of view that's a big step – a positive one.

One of the things you can learn from this is that you are not doing your life. This clearly happened to you and you didn't do anything. Whatever is happening might continue or it might stop and you go back to your old identity. But you won't have much to do with that.

I know what to do to bring the feeling back, but it just seems too radical. I have to let go and let the universe take over my body. I feel scared.

The reality is that the universe has always taken over your body – but you thought that you were in charge of it. That was a wrong idea. Probably last week you saw that and you relaxed into it and let existence run the show.

Yes, but only because everything was so good. You say that the old way is total illusion, but I'm not sure that I've seen that.

Well, maybe not after just a few meetings, but it seems that you've understood something because you were affected by the energy of those few meetings. Even though you didn't understand that this is all an illusion, within yourself you understood something deeply and you were able to come into the energy of the meetings. When something is touched in you, you start to see a new possibility. This is really beautiful, because having even a glimpse like that totally changes your life.

If you live in a house with ten rooms, that's the limit of your universe and you don't even have any imagination that there might be more. Then one day you happen to open a door and find a staircase leading to ten more rooms upstairs. 'Wow, that's fantastic!'

It always touches me when people have a glimpse because I know how beautiful it is. I also know that once you've had a glimpse you are somehow 'finished', because it is going to change your mind. You now know something that you didn't know before. It is so beautiful, so blissful, that it's impossible to ignore it.

After some months the woman came back to another retreat we were holding at the house and again she had a strong opening. This time I talked to her soon after it happened.

Could you say what's happening now?

Actually, there is nothing to say. Nothing ever happened. I think it's not necessary to worry about anything because it is all delusion.

Your face looks as if you don't worry too much. There's really a softness and a happiness in your face.

I don't worry at all! And it feels really good! No judgments. Nothing. I'm so relaxed. There are thoughts, but I think they are not so dangerous. They come and they pass. There is such a lot of space! I can't describe it. Such silence!

Can you find anything that we might call 'desire' going on inside you? Is there anything you want?

Wants, no. No great wishes.

You feel very contented, peaceful?

Yes. It's like that.

All the time?

Yes, all the time.

Do you have any sense of yourself 'doing' something for this opening? Did you do something that contributed to it or did it just happen?

I don't know exactly. It was a great surrender. A few years ago I started meditating. After only a few times I was in silence. I started looking for support. I read a lot of books and I did my meditation. Maybe it would still have happened if I had done nothing. I don't know.

One of the key things about meditation is that we look inside. We take our whole focus from the outside – from expecting something from the world – and we bring the energy towards the inside. What you're really saying is there is deep acceptance of what is.

Yes. Judgments and desires have simply fallen away.

I can remember sitting quietly alone in my apartment in India many years ago. I was looking out at the trees and listening to the birds. The sun was shining. For no obvious reason there was suddenly an amazing flash, like a flash of lightning. It was like a flame of immense energy inside – what I would call bliss. It was my first conscious glimpse and had immense power. Glimpses like that happened at various times in my life, but that one was the first and the strongest relative to my previous state of consciousness. It was also particularly beautiful. The first glimpse feels very dramatic because we go from being closed to suddenly being completely open.

For the glimpse to continue and to ground inside you, it is important that your body is prepared. I spent about sixteen years doing a lot of meditation, body work, energy work and Tai Chi on a regular basis, which all contributed to my energy system opening up. There was also a lot of singing and dancing, and through it all my body became more and more open. I couldn't really judge that for myself, but if I look back now I would say that there were definitely some dramatic changes.

When this glimpse happens and for a few moments or a few hours or even for a few days you see more about who you really are, all the issues, problems and suffering in your life completely disappear. They are replaced by an amazing sense of emptiness and peace, and you immediately recognise this as something you have always longed for. It's 'home', and you immediately know that. It's deeply touching, and it's almost impossible to forget.

Unfortunately, we've set up a society that is constantly asserting the mundane, so people do in fact forget it. But nevertheless, for many it becomes a reason to change. It can be a reason to make new priorities, or the old priorities just don't work anymore. This is a very profound moment. I remember a very serious seeker sitting in front of my spiritual master, Papaji, saying, 'Well, I had a little bit of enlightenment.' Papaji said, 'That's enough. A little bit is enough!' He meant that once you've had this taste you can't leave it anymore. You are ready to change your life.

Papaji was my direct final master. He was the catalyst for a life-changing moment of realising the Self. I stayed with him for nearly five years after that. He stayed in Lucknow from 1989 until he passed away in 1997. Many came to sit with him and many stayed on to realise the Self.

A glimpse has the value of keeping the longing and passion going, but it can also be a hindrance because there is a tendency to want to have the same experience over and over again. There is a Satsang phenomenon where people come to get a kind of high. They leave the meeting feeling very open and empty. Being present leads to experiencing oneness and love. Maybe they get the idea that the good feeling comes from the teacher, but that's not true. It comes from being present.

Of course it is useful to go to these meetings, but it is also important to understand what is really happening. It is very easy to get caught up in feeling good, but understanding can easily be hindered by feelings such as ecstasy or peace. People can become dependent on the teacher or on the meetings and they are not really ready to change. If you really want to wake up there has to be a willingness to experience new things. You may have to go through some very uncomfortable moments.

People who have had a glimpse often say that they feel very vulnerable for some time because they no longer have any ideas to hang on to. Before, you had your ideas and your drama and you thought that was you. But now it's changing and you're moving towards a new realisation of who you are. You wanted this and now it's happening. That's very clear, but it doesn't necessarily make you feel good because it won't feel good until you are through the transition. You'll have good moments, but during this transition time you won't feel so grounded. You might not feel so sure. You won't just be able to respond and perhaps you'll feel insecure. Part of you still remembers the old and you haven't quite come to the new yet.

You don't have the ready answers you had before. All your previous reactions came from your old conditioning and now you don't have a response because you haven't had time to become familiar with your new position. This new position will be you. It will come from you, not from what people told you.

> *'Just relax,' the hospital staff kept telling Jim, but it was to no avail. Jim's wife was in labor and Jim was a nervous wreck. After what seemed like a week, to both Jim and the hospital staff, a nurse came out with the happy news, 'It's a girl,' she cried.*
> *'Thank God! A girl,' said Jim. 'At least she won't have to go through what I just went through!'*

It will be all your own thing. Authentic behaviour can seem strange and unpredictable in comparison to the behaviour that is generally expected in society. Going from being robotic to being a free individual who is responding spontaneously to what's happening is an enormous and beautiful transition. To achieve a new understanding is not so difficult. To bring this new understanding into your daily life it is very supportive to have had a glimpse, a knowing of who you are.

Tales of Awakening
Sharing Moments of Liberation

Since I began sharing fifteen years ago I have met many people who have had a spontaneous glimpse of satori or awakening. Many have been my students and normally the opening has happened around Self-enquiry, Who am I? Sharing this opening has always been a joyous moment, even if later it disappears.

During public meetings people often speak about opening experiences. For many, the initial peace and joy is later replaced by much anguish when they 'lose' it. Some never understand what is happening and fear that they are suffering a mental breakdown. Sometimes friends go away and they are left isolated.

When a strong energy phenomenon occurs it is not necessarily a spiritual opening. We have made a film, *Satori*, which shows a direct, real-life example of a spiritual opening. There is a trailer of that film on the DVD in the back of this book. The stories of satori or awakening glimpses in this chapter and in the film provide much-needed information about this increasingly familiar phenomenon.

A spiritual opening can be a full awakening or satori, or when the opening is for a short time I call it a glimpse. For a full awakening or satori the important criterion is that the sense of a separate identity, what is called the ego, 'me', dissolves. The mind is likely to become quiet and a sense of wellbeing and peace permeates the body-mind entity. With a glimpse, the identification returns after a short time and often brings a sense of anguish or sadness that peace has been lost.

Juergen

Juergen is a computer software designer from Nuremberg. He was thirty-six when I first met him, and it was soon clear that he had one of those minds that works five times faster than anybody else's. He had been meditating and studying Reiki for two years and he came to my retreat in India, where the focus is always on Self-enquiry. When he arrived home after four weeks away, he was met by a very unexpected situation. Just after this, Juergen shared what happened.

The day I came back from India, my wife, whom I've known for half my life, sat down with me at the table for dinner. We hadn't been there five minutes when she said, 'Oh, by the way, I had a love affair while you were away.' Very interesting! We have a son who is three years old. We have a nice apartment and a very well organised and very beautiful life and all of a sudden also a lover.

We had both been really looking for Truth for some time and actually we both knew that this area of relationship had a big potential for stories and dramas. Now I know that just the word 'relationship' is already a story, but back then it was really a very serious topic. We had spoken several times about how it might be if there was ever a lover, but there is a very big difference between talking about it and it really happening. And all of a sudden there he was – the lover!

Because of my four weeks in India with Premananda I was really well prepared for any impossible situation! I knew about Self-enquiry and I had had four weeks to really perfect it! But over the next two weeks I watched as my mind started going completely crazy, telling incredible bullshit. 'Why him? What does he have that I don't? What about the child? What about the apartment? Who gets the car and who gets the cupboards?' It was all bullshit and I knew it, but still my mind just produced this stuff.

Then there was this wonderful evening where I was sitting in the corner on my couch with a cup of tea, totally caught up in all the stories my mind was telling me. The more drama the mind produced the greater was the urge to do something – anything, maybe leave, call the divorce lawyer, throw out my wife or shoot the lover!

But instead I was just sitting there in the corner of the couch doing Self-enquiry, and as it got worse and worse there was this one really important moment where something inside me asked the question, 'What would be the truth if the mind would just shut up?' Then the incredible answer came, 'I would be sitting on the couch, just like thousands of times before, with a cup of tea in my hand.'

All of a sudden everything changed. Everything that was in my mind was just not true, didn't have anything to do with truth, nothing. In that moment I could see it so clearly that everything just fell down, collapsed like a building in that second. Since then the mind sometimes tells stories, but there's nobody left who is actually taking it seriously or who is listening. This is a very important point because some people think that awakened people always have completely still minds. But actually, the point is that they know that what happens in the mind doesn't have anything to do with them. It is the same with the feelings and with the body. All that remains is consciousness, and that is infinite freedom and peace.

Before that moment you were identified with all the thoughts and dramas that were happening in your mind, but when the identification dropped you saw and experienced the Truth of what remained.

The point is that before this moment there was somebody who cared about it. The difference between 'sadness just being there' and 'somebody being sad' is huge. All the questions about why is this happening to me or why is this happening at all relate to a person to whom this stuff happens. Afterwards, stuff is just there and there's not even a question of why. There is no pain or misery left. Together with this 'I', the idea that there is somebody who could do something or change something drops away. The whole perspective changes to just being an observer of every moment.

Juergen started to do Self-enquiry and suddenly it became clear that nothing was happening. There was a body sitting on the couch and a mind freaking out. In that moment he really understood.

Six months after this meeting he wrote the following email:
The mind-body entity Juergen is only awareness. The world is totally gone – nothing is real. There is only awareness. Nothing else. Nothing ever happened. Nothing is left but awareness. Awareness of what? Awareness of nothing.

In the last months some beliefs in a world that is real must have still been there. For sure there was this amazing awareness of everything, but one wonderful point was missed until today: that there is really nothing accept awareness. Really nothing. Awareness is all there is. Everything that pops up in this awareness does not exist. Nothing is real. Nothing. Only awareness exists. Only awareness is. Oh, my God! Oh, my God! Juergen is totally gone. Nothing left. Consciousness, awareness, love, existence, Self, God, Premananda, Juergen – all the same. All one. All awareness. I am out of words. At the moment even the body cannot move. Fingers are working on a keyboard. An awareness of fingers working on a keyboard. No fingers, no keyboard, just awareness. Nothing ever happened. Nothing exists. It is in all of the books but now it is. Awareness of never-ending gratefulness. Awareness of bliss.

Since then he has been helping many people, talking to them and giving support. His whole life has become focused on Truth, and still he is maintaining his successful computer software design business. He is still a very good father to his son and a much better husband to his wife. He doesn't mind that his wife and her boyfriend are having a love affair. There is nobody to mind.

This was the situation until one year after his awakening when suddenly he announced he was no longer interested in meeting with me. Six years have passed since then without any contact.

Susan

Susan had an outwardly successful life. She was a homeopath and was happily married to a handsome doctor. They had a prosperous life together, and nothing seemed to be missing. However, something gradually changed inside her as she began to feel she wanted more depth in her life. There was something else, and she wanted to follow her curiosity to find out what that was. So she left her husband and her comfortable married life and moved into an apartment, alone, in a different city.

As she unpacked her books she noticed a very old copy of a book by Ramana Maharshi. It had been in her collection for some years but she had not been drawn to it before. As she read it she found herself completely interested and pulled to explore further. From there she found out about Satsang, about me and about Self-enquiry and how to apply it in her life.

I did Self-enquiry intensely twenty-four hours a day over many weeks. After some time I noticed that it took on a life of its own. I applied Self-enquiry to everything I did or experienced in my daily life. It took me away from the world out there – which we think is real – back to the source, to where the world comes from. I was very gentle with myself because some really strong things came up. Doubts and resistance will come, you can be sure about that.

I had already realised that I had quite old ideas and habits in my life. I thought I had problems with making decisions, then, during the Summer Retreat, Premananda was telling a story and I asked a question. We went into a very intense dialogue. I felt something inside being released, like a knot. Something was understood on a very deep level and it was very liberating. Looking back, I can see that was an important moment for me because I always thought that 'I' had to make the decisions in my life.

In that moment in Satsang there was suddenly an enormous

presence, and it felt like leaving the body, at an enormous distance. Consciousness was seeing this body projected onto itself. For forty-two years I had identified myself with this body and the story of Susan, and in that moment I realised that it was not me, that it couldn't be me. I could only laugh. There was no doubt. This consciousness — that which was seeing what was happening — is so familiar. It is wonderful. There are no words for it.

It was so clear that I was not the body with all its ideas, games and entanglements. My life has changed drastically since then because I know that there isn't anybody that something could ever happen to, who could get punished or hurt. That's the Truth and it's very, very simple. I am nobody special. It can happen to anybody.

Since my awakening a lot has changed in relation to my friends and family. Actually my whole life has changed. I had been living in Berlin but I gave everything up and moved into the community, the only place that made sense for me to be. This awakening process was initiated already quite some time before, but after the awakening I withdrew myself more as I was more interested in being with myself than relating with others. Then, of course, as I was not in touch or even very interested in all the happenings of my friends and family they began avoiding and excluding me. Be glad about it, because the gift that you are getting is beyond words.

Self-enquiry really helped to get some distance from 'my' stuff. Even after the first week it was clear to me that I am not the thoughts, feelings and sensations, and through continuing the Self-enquiry this distance became greater and I came more and more into silence and stillness, and more into the present.

Watching yourself in the present and doing Self-enquiry dissolves all the boundaries because you become aware of all that binds you — everything that keeps you from being present. You have to be honest and really want to see it.

Someone recently asked me if I still experienced emotions. Of course I still have feelings, but I'm not identified with them. They are there, but in that moment I enjoy them. Usually the feelings depend on stories, the story of the past and the story of the future. The stories belong to the conditioned mind, but that doesn't exist anymore in my life so there is much more space to just capture the moment, to realise the moment.

There isn't anybody any more who wants to become anything or who can decide anything. It's already decided and there is openness for whatever there is. Everything that happens, happens anyway, but if you have a conditioned mind then you think that you are the one who's doing it.

My experience is that when you have a longing to really, really wake up and to get rid of all the dramas and the stories of the conditioned mind, existence will definitely help you.

Birgit

Birgit grew up in a household where she was never allowed to express her feelings and where her parents used old-fashioned punishments, like locking her up in the basement for being naughty.

When she was eighteen she had a boyfriend who she loved very much. One day he rode off on his motorbike to get cigarettes but had an accident and did not survive. She could never show any grief to her parents, and all they would say was, 'Why do you have to cry?'

She was a very intelligent young woman and she became a computer specialist, working as the head of a department at an Internet provider. Her incredibly detailed mind was perfect for this kind of work.

After her awakening glimpse she came to live with us in the community and shared her experience with us.

I went for a two-week holiday to the Canary Islands and I was alone the whole time, doing Self-enquiry. Everything was really beautiful. It was so peaceful, there was so much love and I was simply the ocean.

My whole life long I had a kind of problem, which was that I didn't want to live; I wanted to die. It became a problem because everybody

Awake and Free

around me was saying that it was not normal to have the wish to die and my family took me to psychiatrists. So I did lots of therapy, which of course never helped. Anyway, I did some other things and the issue became somehow less dramatic and in the last couple of years this wish to die has rarely surfaced.

During the holiday I was lying in bed one night and feeling really, really happy and suddenly – whoosh!! – everything went black. The only thing left was this enormous wish to die, exactly how it had been in the past. It came with an immense power. It felt like a huge black storm raining down on me. But what was different from before, and what didn't surprise me, was that there was no drama; it didn't bother me. It was simply there.

For a short moment I was a bit curious about why it wasn't a drama anymore but then already the next moment came and everything changed. Everything became white because I suddenly realised why I wanted to die, or what this wish to die really was. It was simply letting go of the story so that everything I felt attached to finally dropped away.

It was that all this nonsense, all these old stories, all the old rubbish we always carry along, this whole 'me' simply died, stopped, full stop, finished! It was such a relief, tears where running down my cheeks and I was happy in a way I never had been before. In that moment it simply dropped and since then it hasn't come back. No old stories anymore, no thoughts, no touchy feelings, no 'I'. Thank God.

You're working in an Internet company and you are in charge of a small department where you do very demanding technical work. Can you still manage all this difficult technical stuff?

Yes, better than before, and it also works better because it doesn't really matter anymore.

What would you say to everyone right now?

Wake up!

What does 'wake up' mean? Because actually right now everyone thinks they are awake. They're wearing their awake clothes and their pyjamas are under their pillows.

Yes, that's true. But if you look at what's happening around you and you believe that this is true, then you know you are dreaming.

Would you say that waking up is actually quite simple?

I don't know. In my case it was easy. I didn't do anything.

What about all this Self-enquiry on the rocks?

Well, I also did it because I enjoyed it so much. Self-enquiry gave me little insights. There is no answer to the question 'who am I?' and every time I experienced that there is no answer, I then experienced whatever was there – blackness or peace or whatever.

The fire is burning. You can see it in my red ears and my red cheeks – it is so beautiful. There is trust that whatever is seemingly happening is just right. Quite some people have asked me recently if I have fallen in love. I always say yes, because basically it is very similar. When you fall in love you let everything go and nothing else exists anymore, and that's what it's like in awakening. Nothing else is important. It's simply divine. And so simple.

Recently I was looking into the eyes of a ten-year-old girl and it became so clear in this moment that the only thing we are, and the only thing that exists at all, is God. You can call it love or pure consciousness or the Self; it doesn't matter. Everything else is rubbish.

Patricia

Patricia has been living with me for about four years now. She came to a point in her life where she had done a lot of inner work, through therapy, workshops and theatre, for example, but there was never a focus on spirituality. She led a very normal life, raising a daughter, working in regular jobs, going through relationships. However, she never lost contact to something inside her, which on some level was reminding her that there was more, or that what she was looking for on the outside would not ultimately fulfil her.

Very recently, she experienced a strong spiritual opening in the main office of Open Sky House, at the end of a very normal day while she was typing an email. It became clear that there was a very strong energetic phenomenon happening to her. Without any doubt she had a glimpse of her true nature. As she has had several glimpses there is a sense that this time it is an awakening or satori.

Later I invited Patricia to share her experience about this awakening, but also to share how she had been unknowingly preparing herself for something deeper to happen. On the day of her awakening experience, I had an appointment in the city and I took her to translate for me. Afterwards we had a coffee in a near-by cafe and later she drove me back home. Were you already aware of something happening at this point?

I don't know when it exactly was, but I know when I was driving back I felt something like a lot of energy around my heart and I thought, 'Hmm! I wonder if this is the second cappuccino!'

Back in the community I was working in the office and the energy got stronger and stronger. I went to a mirror to see my eyes, because I had the feeling that they were two huge burning balls. I looked in the mirror and saw these big, amazing eyes.

Then I went back to my desk and I had the feeling, 'It can't be only the cappuccino!' I sat down in front of my computer, but then a lot of energy came into my arms and they started cramping up – I couldn't write anymore. I thought, 'When you have a heart attack you have pain in the arms.' But I had no pain, and nothing felt threatening, so I just surrendered to what was happening. I had the feeling I might fall off the chair.

I didn't know what it was but I wasn't really worried. There was enormous energy going on, especially in the arms – they cramped, and I couldn't move them – and then the whole body was like on an electric chair. I didn't have any control anymore over my body.

At that time I was already in the room. It didn't look particularly lovely or blissful or sweet, it was more like you were going through a birth. There was a sense that you were actually birthing yourself!

I have given birth, and the similarity with this experience is that it just carries you along. In birth, once the contractions start it takes you over and the whole process continues without you doing anything. That part was exactly the same. There was such a strong energy suddenly entering the body that all I could do was let everything happen.

What was happening was a huge energy phenomenon. Most people's bodies are not ready for that, and that's why it often closes down quite quickly. But this is the third or fourth time this has happened to you, and you're a very open woman.

When you opened your eyes during this experience, what was that like? How did you see things?

I remember things looked amazing; it must be similar to how babies see things. I was looking at a little lump of paint on the ceiling and it was so fascinating, like being on LSD. My eyes were completely absorbed in it. It was completely amazing.

There was a point when you started laughing uncontrollably. What was going on then?

I remember hearing laughing, and I thought it sounded like my sister when we were teenagers and used to giggle on for hours and hours. I thought, 'Amazing! Where's this laughter coming from? Is she here laughing?' Suddenly I realised it was me laughing, or rather I was this laughing. That was very interesting because I was out of the body and the laughing was just happening. Then suddenly it was me laughing.

What did you feel the next day?

I was very touched by the community and how they had supported me. There were about six people who gathered in the room when they heard about what was happening. I wasn't so aware of that, but I knew there were people around and I just felt that I was very well cared for, with the people holding me and giving me water. I could feel the love from everybody in the office, and the silence of everyone sitting on the floor between the computers, shelves and chairs. It was very beautiful.

I talked to Patricia two weeks later to find out what was going on for her.

It feels more quiet and silent, a deeper quality of quietness than before. It's really a beautiful thing. It's very subtle and in a way very unspectacular. It's soft and sweet.

When I close my eyes I feel a lot of energy moving. When I walk around I don't feel it so much, but when I close my eyes, especially for a longer time, I feel it strongly.

And can you function well in everyday life?

I can't function so well. It's quite one dimensional. It works well on a basic level; I can do one thing after the other, but if three people come at once to ask questions and the phone starts ringing, the energy of the situation really feels like it's penetrating the body. There is a strong sense of being vulnerable because my energy system is so open, but this openness is actually very lovely.

At the time of writing four months have passed and the satori continues to deepen. Patricia functions well day by day, continuing to organise the community, drive to her part-time clowning job and run the community seminar business. She experiences a quiet mind, an easy flow of her life and a big yes to what ever happens. Things are uncomplicated and easy.

Living in Freedom
Paradise Now

It's Monday evening and nothing particular has happened all day. We had some guests come for breakfast; we cleaned the house, fed the animals and sent some emails. Now we come together at the end of the day, a very normal day, and meet in Satsang. We sit in silence and are just present, feeling the chairs beneath us, the carpet under our feet and hearing the odd sound. It's actually very ordinary.

If I asked you why you're reading this book right now, I wonder what answers I would get. Perhaps something like, 'I want to wake up', 'I want to be free' or 'I would like to live in true happiness.' All of this we can loosely call enlightenment or awakening.

Then, of course, I would ask you what you mean by enlightenment. What is your idea about it? Probably a lot of people want enlightenment because they would like to be happy all the time and they would like everything that isn't so nice in their lives to stop and be replaced by piles of ice-cream!

I don't know what expectations you might have, but actually enlightenment is very ordinary. It would be much more honest to say you become ordinary than to say that you become special. You don't become Superman, you become just as you are. It may well be that who you are is actually Superman, but it might also be quite ordinary.

The life of any so called 'awakened' person looks just like anybody else's life. They might do some gardening, wash the dishes, drive a car or go for a walk, and they probably eat sometimes! They do all the same stuff that everybody else does.

From a perspective of 'me' it's difficult to imagine how anyone could live *not* from 'me', but from an awakened person's point of view it is completely ordinary. The 'expression' is the same for everyone.

The difference is inside – somebody who is awakened has come to see the nature of the Self. They have overcome the identification with the false self, the ego.

If you are busy with your concepts, your ideas, your beliefs, you are identifying with being separate. You are trying to control or manipulate your life to get what 'I' want; you are trying to be happy. Somebody who is awakened, on the other hand, is in harmony with the unfolding of life – whatever it brings.

We have a new resident in the community. When I first met her as an occasional visitor to Satsang, she was especially curious as to how awakened people live. The idea of living without the 'me' was fascinating for her, which is probably one of the strong reasons why she became interested in the spiritual path in the first place.

This morning I passed through the office to check how she was settling in. After a chat about the project she was newly working on and how she was doing in general, she took the opportunity to ask about my life and how I experienced it free from the 'I', the false identity.

Premananda, do you practise what you preach? What does it mean to live without the constant reference to 'me' and what 'I' want?

Well, without this reference point there is a blank canvas. From the emptiness, living, work and play express in a very spontaneous way. I don't even know what the next words will be – I'm interested to find out!

You just said you live from emptiness. What do you exactly mean by that?

I mean that I have stepped out of the illusion that I am somebody, a somebody who has a story and a somebody who experiences everything from this separate being, 'me'. In a single moment I came to see that it was simply not true, and just by itself this illusion fell away. Nothing really changed but there is no longer this sense of a separate somebody.

Being in the now, stories of the past and the future don't arise and this gives an enormous space for love. The basic space inside is emptiness, peace, stillness, love, and everything is perceived from the divinity and beauty of that space. The world doesn't disappear into a grey nothing. The awakened person sees and perceives the world not so differently from anybody else. The difference is that the world no longer appears as external and separate but as the Self.

Does this include everyday life? How do you perceive that?

In every ordinary thing there is amazement. When I walk through the courtyard I often stop and look at a little bird or a rabbit or the ducks. I often go and look at the chickens in the garden. They are just doing what rabbits or birds or chickens do – it's completely ordinary stuff – but it always touches me. I have a room with windows onto the Rhine and every time I look out I am completely touched. The seasons are always changing and the trees, the sunset, the ships and the level of the river are always a bit different. It's always alive and it's always beautiful.

Many years ago these things wouldn't have really moved me. I would have just seen a river or trees or animals because my mind was never really here to perceive anything. There was an attitude of 'the good stuff will come later – in the future'. To be here and just accept everything as it is makes every ordinary thing extraordinary.

So when I called your name earlier in the courtyard and you turned to look at me, who turned? Who responded?

Whatever is here responds to that name. Maybe for you it's very simple. You look over here and you see an old, slightly fatty English guy so you think, 'Okay, that must be Premananda.' You've got a kind of identity kit functioning that creates a picture about him.

Then what about over here? What would be over here when you called 'Premananda'? On a simple kind of material level we're separate. It seems like something over here, 'me', is recognising something over there, 'you', which is outside of 'me'.

Maybe it's not so easy to understand but if I look at what is here I can say there is nothing here. There is a 'nothing' sitting, there is a 'nothing' responding to the name. That is perhaps not the right word, for how can 'nothing' respond? So then what word to use? We could try 'the beloved' or 'consciousness'. I could say 'consciousness' responds to the name, but it doesn't help you to understand.

Can you please say something about the difference between 'being' and 'doing'? I'm confused, because on one hand I can understand intellectually that there is only 'being' but on the other hand I see you and everyone else in the community 'doing' a lot.

If I look back on the last few hours I can see that things just happen – not really according to any plan. 'Being' has a different flavour to 'doing'. A lot can be happening but it comes from a flow and has nothing to do with an idea of making something happen. Things happen unexpectedly.

Last night I picked up my phone to call somebody in Australia and in that moment they sent me a text message. It was six-thirty in the morning in Australia, so I wouldn't particularly expect that person to be available. These little synchronicities are quite normal in 'being', but they don't appear in 'doing'. Life is more unexpected, and, whatever the situation, it always has some feeling of 'alright'. When there is no real idea, life becomes a series of happenings.

Do you feel you act from your personality?

Yes. Everyone has a personality. The difference is that an awakened person knows that this is not who he or she is. My direct master, Papaji, was a natural boss who took charge in any situation. Osho had a playful, adventurous character, liking variety and choice. In his ashram he offered many kinds of meditations.

Is there fear in your being?

Do I have fear? Ah, yes! I'm afraid somebody will eat my chocolates – but then I could get some more, so it's not a big fear! Seriously, I can't think of any fears, and it's been like that for years. Of course it's beautiful to live without fear, but you get used to it and then it's just normal. Part of the reason for not having fear is that I just deal with what life presents each day. The other part is that there is not an attachment to being a separate somebody.

Can you imagine living without suffering, without worries, jealousies, fears? Can you imagine what it could be like if they all just fell away? I haven't been jealous for twenty years; I haven't had fear or any problems for twenty years. If you drop everything that preoccupies you almost every day and every moment, then what are you going to do? Suddenly you have so much time. You are free of all the nonsense.

There may be an emotion in the present moment – sadness or anger. There may be a thought, and of course some planning is necessary. Everything comes and it goes. In one sense not much is different and in another sense everything is different because there is naturally trust and spontaneity. I live from moment to moment in the joy of the unknown, the unknowable.

Can you describe it?

It is so difficult to talk about but when it happens you know immediately; you completely know it. Once you eat a piece of chocolate you absolutely know what chocolate tastes like, but try explaining the taste to someone who has not experienced it. You can try of course, but nobody could know the taste of chocolate just from your explanation.

Living in Freedom

When we start with spiritual transformation there seem to be so many things we can do. There are many different techniques, meditations and diets. There is a huge variety of exercises including Tai Chi, Yoga, Qigong and special breathing techniques. It isn't long before we have the idea that if we keep doing all these things they will bring us to freedom. Unfortunately they don't. The deeper and greater understanding is that there is nothing to do – nothing. If you want to win the Tour de France you have to practise relentlessly. Unfortunately, it's not like that if you want to be free. At a certain point, 'doing' doesn't help you anymore. In fact, at a certain point it is in the way; it sabotages you. It is a subtle balance. Consciousness is intelligent. If we make ourselves available to this intelligence it supports us.

When we're young we feel the pressure of achieving goals and trying to understand the point of our lives, but a big discovery is to realise that life has no point. Your mind wants it to have a point, but if you really investigate it you won't be able to find one. If there is a point you could say it would be to find out who you are, but once you know who you are – then what? You still have to have breakfast, and you still have to cook lunch and wash your clothes. Unfortunately, awakening doesn't come with a private servant and other such perks. You have to live your life just as before.

In one way, nothing really changes – except that everything is very simple and you don't have to find something special in order to be content. The reality is that you're content all the time. Really seeing this creates a strange situation, because suddenly you discover that actually there's nothing that can make you feel good. You can play games like, 'Ah! Chocolate is good; ice-cream is good,' but actually everything is good. Even without anything, 'being' is good!

You have to be a little bit careful what you project about awakening or enlightenment. If you think you're going to get little wings at the back and start flying around, it probably won't happen. In my own life, from the age of about twenty-five until I was about fifty, I always had a deep, searching question. I could never really relax and it was always tormenting my life.

Then suddenly – literally from one moment to the next – this completely disappeared. It took some time to absorb that change because for forty-five years there was always a reason, there was always a point. Then suddenly there was no point.

It is a shift in one's perception. It's hard to talk about it because we are all identified with our false self. When you awaken that identification completely collapses, so at the beginning you can feel quite shaky and vulnerable.

When you are under the spell of the false self and somebody talks to you about how you are creating your own world, it doesn't really make much sense to you because your life is just completely natural and automatic. You always did that and you have no way of getting any other sense of it. But when you become Self-realised then you can get a very good sense of it because everything collapses.

The emptiness, the joy of the unknown, is the same in everyone. The only question is whether we are in contact with it or not. Ordinary human beings live much better than the kings of old, and with our survival pretty much taken care of, what then? We are trying to understand, on a very deep level, the meaning of our lives. This is all made a little more difficult because we have spiritual super stars like Jesus Christ, Krishna and Buddha, and in modern times a whole host of gurus and saints.

Their life stories are pretty impressive – walking on water, raising people from the dead. We like our spiritual super stars to have really good stories, but personally I don't buy them. There is no real difference between Buddha and yourself. In essence, everyone is capable of creating themselves into a Buddha. I don't doubt that someone like Buddha or Jesus came to a deep understanding of their true nature, but rather than putting them on a pedestal I would like to see them as a reminder that I too can come to that understanding.

> *A man has his car full of penguins. He drives past a policeman, but the policeman stops him. He says. 'Hey, you! Yes, you! You should take those penguins to the zoo!'*
> *The next day in the same spot, the man still has the penguins.*

Living in Freedom

Once again he drives past the policeman. 'Hey, I thought I told you to take those penguins to the zoo!'
'I did,' replies the man. 'We had so much fun that we're going to the beach today!'

Nothing is missing! What is really true is just now! We have this moment; that's all. With this understanding life becomes paradise – because you are truly free. Free from everything you call 'me'. The way to live an awakened life is to simply be. There is no goal or even any intention. It is all about nothing.

Just so you keep this in perspective, try carrying a handful of sand in your pocket and every time you get very serious take it out and let it run through your fingers – realising that every grain of sand represents a whole galaxy. There are so many galaxies up there that human beings fade into insignificance.

What is offered in this book is a reminder to investigate for yourself the Truth of human life, in fact all life. Discover you have been lulled into accepting a robotic functioning based on the conditioning to which your mind has been subjected. Entertain the possibility of the attachment to the separate false self dissolving. Understand life has no point other than knowing yourself to be awareness and to enjoy the play of each moment unfolding.

I had dinner in a Chinese restaurant last week with a three-year-old girl and her dad. There were chopsticks in a packet. This was enough to keep her entertained for the whole evening. First she opened the packet, then she put the chopsticks in her apple juice and then she played hitting herself on the head with them. Every gesture was wondrous for her. True awakening means you live a bit like that, putting your chopsticks in the apple juice! In other words, not taking life too seriously and living with lightness, humour and joy.

Open Sky House
International Satsang & Arts Community
An Experiment in Conscious Living

The Open Sky House, International Satsang and Arts Community, is housed in a seventeenth century mansion on the banks of the Rhine between Cologne and Dusseldorf, in a small village. There are four regular weekly Satsangs and Energy Darshan with Premananda. In addition, regular weekend intensives and Retreats are held throughout the year. There is an Arts Programme consisting of painting, music, theatre, sculpture, pottery, clowning, singing and dance.

The residents work together running several businesses within the house: Open Sky Press, Rhine River Guest House, Flow Fine Art Gallery and Open Sky Seminar House. All aspects of work, as well as the ordinary daily life of the community: cooking, childcare, cleaning and personal communication, are used as the background to show the robotic nature of most actions. When there is freedom from habitual reactions and patterns, the mind becomes still.

You are welcome to visit as a Guest or a Volunteer.

www.openskyhouse.org

Left page: *Satsang with Premananda, Park outside the house, Parrots in living room, Premananda at lunch*

Right page: *Community baby, Art gallery opening, Celebration time, Winter view onto the Rhine out of the community front window*

Endpage: *Community garden with log circle, Morning meditation, Courtyard in autumn, Community residents in front of our 17th century mansion*

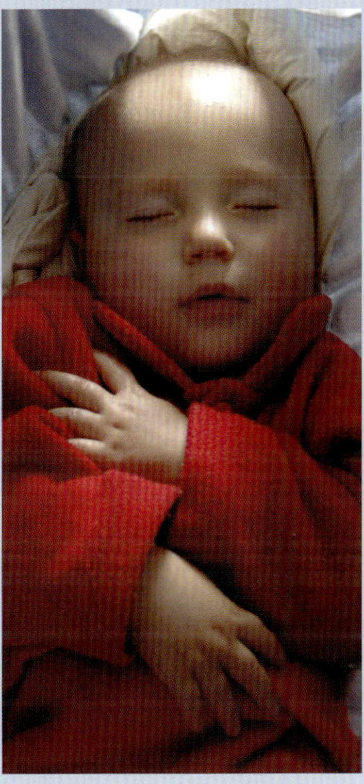

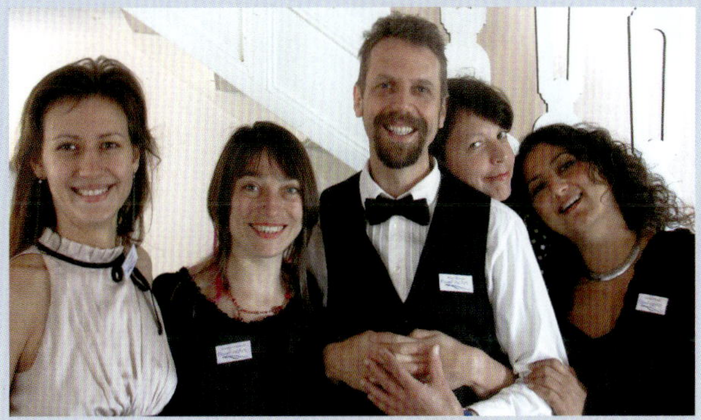

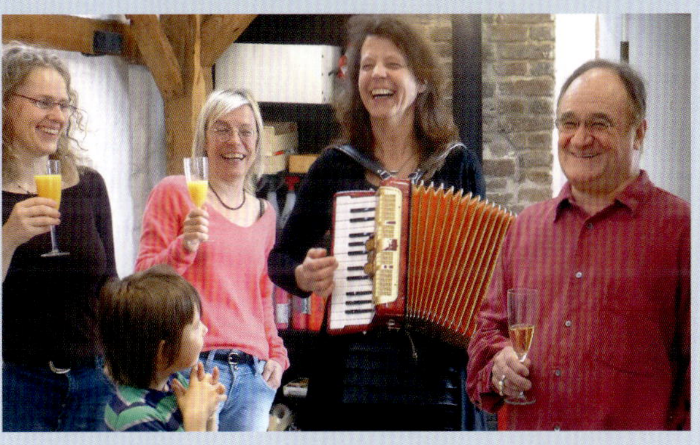

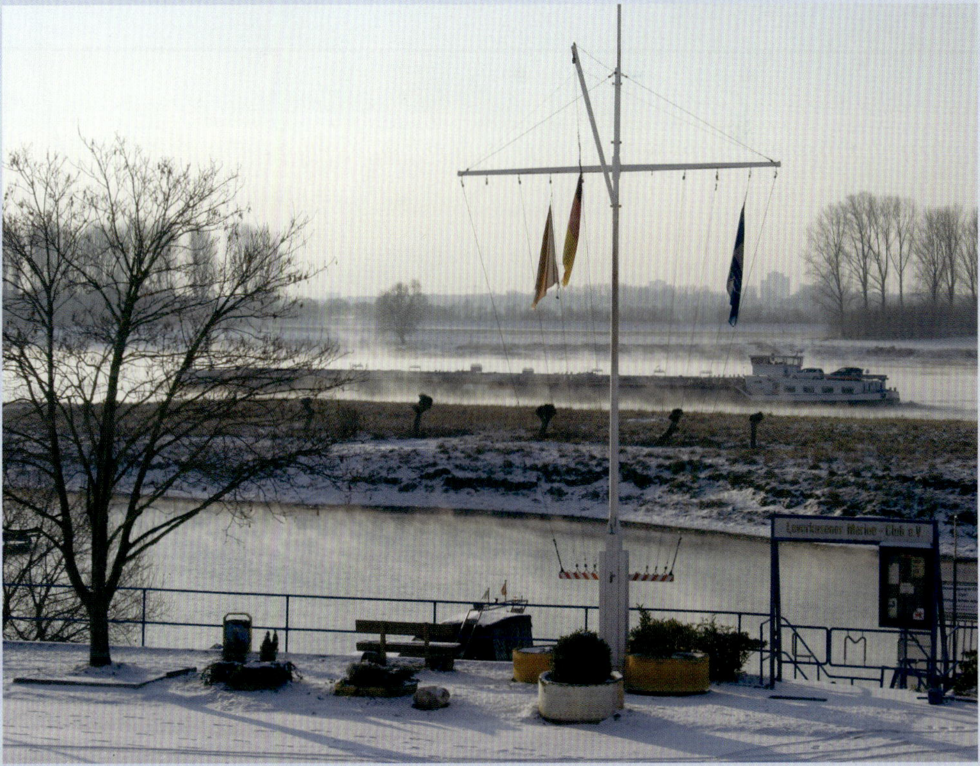

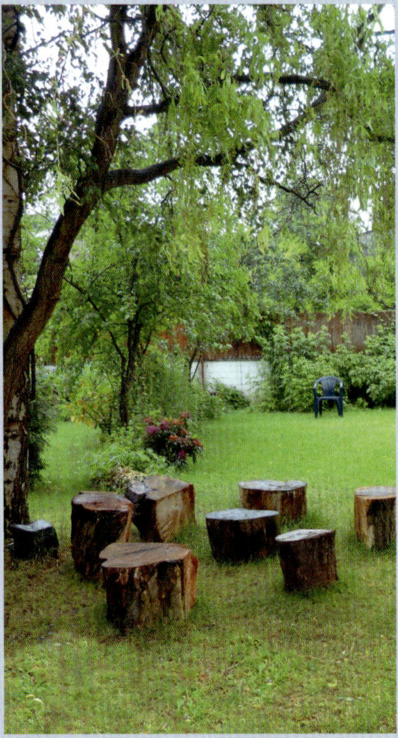

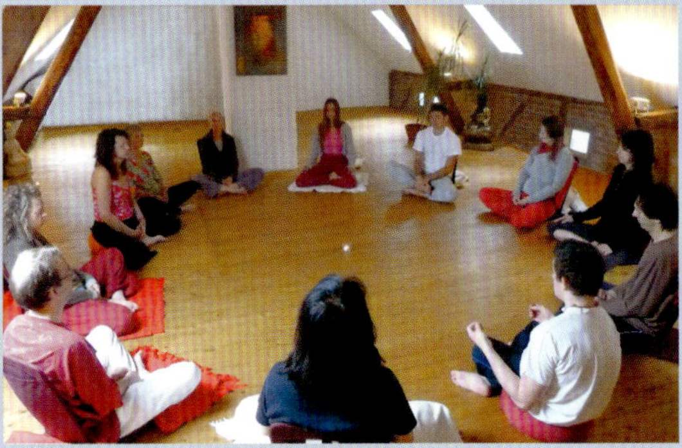

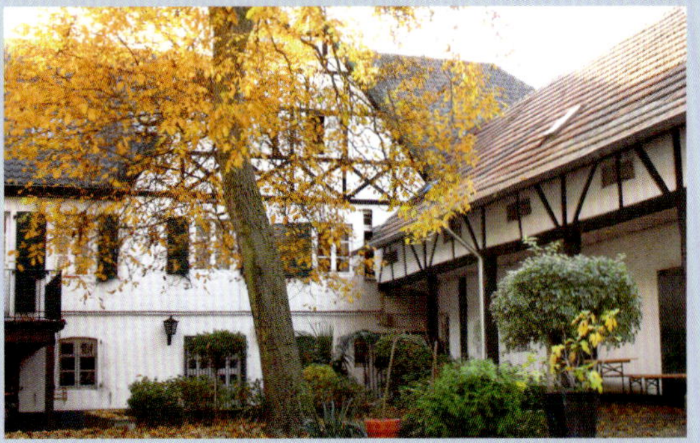

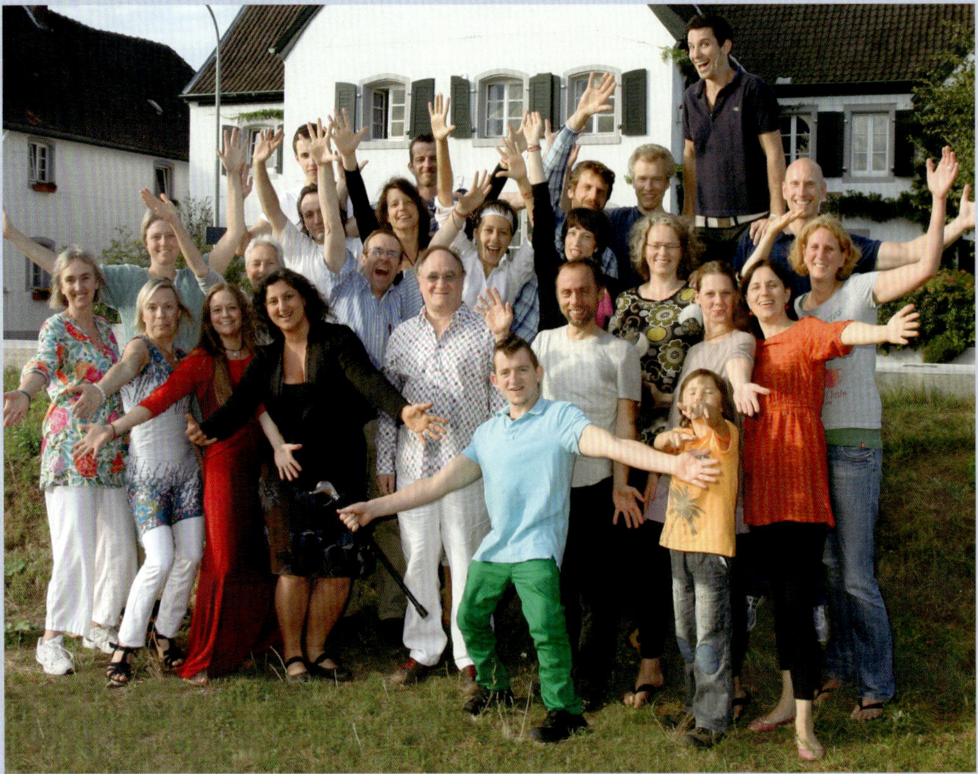

Open Sky House
International Satsang and Arts Community
An Experiment in Conscious Living

The Sangha is a community of people who have the perfect right to cut through your trips and feed you with their wisdom, as well as the perfect right to demonstrate their own neurosis and be seen through by you. The companionship within the Sangha is a kind of clean friendship – without expectation, without demand, but at the same time, fulfilling. True Sangha is only possible within a container of love, intimacy and trust. It takes commitment, willingness, time and patience to create this much-needed environment.

Chögyam Trungpa

The community priority is for spiritual awakening and freedom. The first priority for anyone living here is to find out who he or she is. It is not an esoteric community far removed from life. It is absolutely in life, but awakening is also in life. It is a nice idea that awakening is other than ordinary, but this is not true. Here we continue engaging in ordinary things like cleaning, cooking lunch, taking care of the children, going to work and all the other tasks of any normal household. But at the same time the focus of everything we do is self-awareness.

Open Sky House provides a refuge from the normal restrictions and expectations of society. In this way it creates an open space for those who are really interested to know the Truth of who they are. It is a place where you have the time and support to examine the meaning of your life, and to enquire into who you really are. In most normal working and living situations it is difficult to find the space to look at these questions.

Open Sky House is supported by several in-house businesses that we have created. Our seventeenth century mansion, situated on the banks of the Rhine, makes a perfect guesthouse. Open Sky Press publishes books and films and Open Sky Seminar House utilises the guesthouse and the seminar rooms we have constructed and renovated in various parts of the house and outbuildings. Flow Fine Art Gallery brings beauty into the community. These businesses have all been rather successful and the money from them pays the rent, helps most of the twenty residents to live and develops the community by financing construction projects in the house and other initiatives.

We have developed a studio to transmit most of my meetings through the Internet. Three or four evenings each week the residents translate my English into German, French, Italian, Portuguese, Russian and Spanish as appropriate. They set up the whole studio so we can film and transmit live. It has required them learning lots of new skills and it enables viewers sitting at home in any part of the world to come into the meeting live and dialogue with me. All meetings are available in an archive on the Internet in seven languages.

As all this has developed over the years, I have found myself quite pleased that it has not become an institutionalised monastery or ashram where people live quietly with limited interaction. As well as providing the finances for our projects, the many tasks and situations associated with the businesses give everyone the chance to see the workings of their own mind. The businesses and projects prevent the community becoming divorced from everyday life.

As well as the businesses, the residents work in many different fields. We have a clown, a photographer, musicians, artists, a nurse, a computer programmer and an English teacher to give a few examples. Through it all is the understanding that everyone can awaken. It is absolutely available to everyone. Awakening is our true nature, and in the community we are scraping away the old rubbish in order to reveal this nature.

An Experiment in Conscious Living

People have ideas about what 'spiritual' is, and it has a lot to do with a certain serious kind of silence. We have periods of meditation, of course, and the silence of Satsang, but the silence we are most interested in is not the silence of 'doing' meditation, not something 'spiritual' that you attain. It is a capacity that whatever we are 'doing' is coming from our true nature, which is the deep silence, the emptiness of existence. The whole effort is to embody into daily life any opening that is happening; to become present in the moment, whatever we are doing – running businesses, making phone calls, buying groceries.

We can be very active together, and in the next moment there is tremendous silence. The intention in the community is to remind each other to be present and to watch our robotic behaviours and repeated structures. To this end, we invite someone working closely with us to be our Buddy, giving feedback as they observe our common patterns. There is a sense of the community becoming more conscious and having its own destiny as it moves towards freedom.

In the 1980s I lived in Osho's community in America. It wasn't really a community; it was a small, developing city. There was an airport, a hotel, a bus system. There were about thirty of those old American yellow buses driving around, picking up people and dropping them off, just like a regular bus system in any city. If you saw one of those bus drivers you might ask, 'What is this guy doing driving his bus all day?' I would reply, 'Is he driving the bus, or is he driving himself?' What is his real job? Is he a bus driver? Yes, he drives the bus, but his real work sitting on the bus is to be aware of what is going on inside him. That is his job. His lifestyle is probably completely different from a regular bus driver, but he is also a bus driver.

The person managing our guesthouse didn't come here to be in this role. But by taking it on he gets the opportunity to look at what comes up inside of him when he is doing this job. It is the same for everybody living and working in the community, all contributing in various degrees to the different businesses and projects. They have a valuable opportunity to look inside at what the work brings up.

An open heart is an essential ingredient for looking inside, for accepting yourself, for being open to what is being offered through the mirrors of the community. We see the whole game of work as a kind of service that encourages our hearts to become open. It is not about wanting to get something. In heartfelt service you give, and you trust you will get what you need.

The community is like a laboratory of service, and somewhere along the way each person will meet compassion and humility within themselves. These issues of service, compassion and humility all come back to the heart. The moment you give something – for example in a heartfelt way in service – you can feel it in your chest. All the work we do is contributing to the heart opening.

The overall effect of individual heart openings is for an amazingly powerful field of love to be available to the whole community and guests. It is common for volunteers to arrive closed, even suffering some emotional pain. Then after four or five days they relax and expand. It is always lovely to witness the effect of the community's strong heart energy on guests. It is also available when a resident goes through a difficult time and needs support.

The 'spiritual' work that happens between myself and the residents comes out of our daily contact, out of the daily situations where we work closely together. I have a lot of fun with this! I create situations that remind people of what's happening inside them on a deeper level than they are consciously aware of.

The activity in the house often doesn't make sense. I consciously choose this. I like to create chaos sometimes because it provokes people into exposing structures that may be difficult, uncomfortable to look at or not usually thought of as structures. Being very helpful, for example, can be just as strong a structure as being selfish or greedy.

They are all devices we use, mostly unconsciously, to manipulate our world to get what we want. My job is to shine light on that which has not yet been seen, and chaotic situations give me a chance to see how people function and how I can guide them.

Facing the things that are difficult to see can be confronting. When an openness to look is supported by a loving space you will see

An Experiment in Conscious Living

things about yourself that are difficult to allow, but you may also see something very beautiful. The tremendous love in the community is nourishing and encouraging.

Another role of the work we do is to show how limiting our minds are. We achieve so much more than we would ever imagine possible. With very little experience the residents write books, edit films, run businesses and deal with demanding situations. We manage incredible things that our minds would say were impossible. We humans normally function at a very small percentage of our potential, and one of the effects of the intense activity in the community is that everyone becomes very energised.

When the conditioned mind is not so active and the familiar limitations have less hold on us, there is a great natural energy available. We don't generally notice the mind's limitations and it is only when we take some space and time to focus on this that we see their effects. At Open Sky House many impossible things are achieved before lunch every day.

Everyone in the community wants to know who they are, and they have taken me to be their spiritual teacher. I have accepted that, so we are on a journey together. This creates a totally unique situation. It is a wonderful way to live, offering so much support, and it is an especially wonderful way for a spiritual teacher to live. His whole dream is to find people who are seriously interested in freedom. By surrendering to the teacher you learn to surrender to your own Self, and that brings you out of the structures of the mind and into the flow of life.

Living together with people who have the same focus is an enormous support on the path to Self-realisation. Working together, being together, playing together – every moment is a possibility. Community life provides mirrors that are a constant reminder. They can mirror our emptiness or they can mirror our busyness. If you are ready to look, then the wide range of situations that arise will naturally reveal what you may have chosen to avoid. Also, the many opportunities presented in the community encourage talents and unique skills that might never have been expressed before.

In the eight years of the community there have been two people who have become awakened. They had already been working on themselves before they moved in, but almost certainly the work they did within the community contributed to them ultimately having a moment of Self-realisation. They both came to a point after being some years in the community where they had dealt with many things inside themselves that could have caused difficulties. You could say they went through a grinding and polishing process in the community and in the end there was not so much stuff left to cover up their own being.

Almost everyone in the community has had a glimpse of their true nature, perhaps several times. It is a reminder of what is possible, and a great support and encouragement to continue the inner journey. Every glimpse has the effect of opening that person up a bit more, leaving something behind each time, letting the heart open, letting the old dissolve and accepting what is.

Those who leave before their time, in the sense of leaving without a solid ground of Self-realisation, have left with a greater awareness of what it is that keeps them from the peace of Self-knowledge. There is no doubt that the community over the last eight years has served its intention – a very rare and successful experiment in conscious living.

www.openskyhouse.org

Premananda Biography

After a typical English middle-class upbringing, Premananda found himself in his early twenties working as a structural engineer and later training as an architect, developing his career and enjoying the fruits of life like any ambitious young man. He had a nice apartment, a curvy Beetle, sometimes a girlfriend and a good job in a well-known architectural company in the centre of London. Everything looked pretty set for him to live a comfortable, successful and happy life. His mum was very happy with him.

However, during his teens and early twenties he had developed a question that seemed to be about not knowing what to do with his life, not finding meaning in the world around him. On a deeper inner level he had the strong feeling that he never really fitted in and that he didn't actually want what he had apparently chosen in his life.

One evening he was waiting at an underground station in London during the rush hour, heading back from the centre of town after another long day's work. There was a strong voice inside him that suddenly said this was not the life he wanted. He decided to move abroad, finding an opportunity with an architectural company in Japan.

On his arrival in Tokyo he experienced a huge culture shock and his internal question became even stronger. He again felt this overwhelming sense of not fitting, something he thought he had moved away from by coming abroad. There was something missing in his life, and it brought a great sadness and confusion. He went into a 'dark night of the soul' that lasted several years. He stayed on in Japan because he was engrossed in an internal dialogue that was provoked by being in that alien culture.

The Great Misunderstanding

At twenty-eight Premananda still had no idea about spiritual life, but while in Japan he met a German architecture professor who introduced him to his first master, Osho. At the time he had no interest nor any idea of the significance of the meeting. Twelve months later, through a series of inexplicable events, he arrived at Osho's ashram in Pune, India. As he walked through the gate, which was called 'the gateless gate', he immediately felt at home.

He had found his place. The feeling was emotional, powerful and strong and it was without any reason. It was as if the question he'd had for more than ten years was answered. For the next fifteen years he lived as an Osho sannyasin in India, England and America. Taking part in transformational workshops led to self-awareness, and the years of meditation developed a quiet mind.

Two years after Osho's death, Premananda was living contentedly in Pune when he heard about another teacher, the great Advaita master Sri Harilal Poonja, known to his many devotees as Papaji. He read an interview with this man and also saw a video, but the real interest came when he started noticing people who had come back from visiting him. He saw an amazing transformation in these people. There was a glow and internal smile coming from them that touched him.

Although he had not been looking for another master, he arrived in Lucknow and was surprised by Papaji's enormous availability. Premananda found Papaji almost shockingly available. Shocking, because his immediacy confronted him with the question, 'Why am I here?' He had to really look and question, 'Who am I?' and 'What am I doing here?'

In the first three weeks, Premananda formally sat with Papaji in Satsang each day and three times asked him a question. On the occasion of the third meeting he saw with amazing clarity the thing that, during twenty years of spiritual searching, he had never understood. The Self revealed itself and it was seen that this was his true nature, which had always been known. Without any doubt, that meeting marked a total change in his life. Instantly the identification with Premananda and the story of Premananda were cut. From one moment to the next there was an enormous shift, which can only be described as an awakening to the Self.

Premananda stayed on with his teacher for five years, then he moved to Australia. On the night Papaji left his body Premananda received a powerful energetic internal 'fax' message seemingly from Papaji telling him that he had some work to do. He was incredulous about this, even though the messages continued for two days. At the time he didn't know that Papaji had left his body. This was in 1997 and marked the beginning of Premananda offering Satsang.

At that time Premananda was living in Sydney. He had already collected a group of students for his meditation and Reiki classes. He offered them an informal 'new' kind of meeting. The group expanded rapidly and a building was offered out of the blue. For four years he offered regular Satsang meetings, weekends and retreats in and around Sydney as well as on visits to Melbourne and the Byron Bay area.

Since 2003 Premananda has been based in Germany and travelling widely in Europe, wherever he is invited, illustrating the conditioned mind – the prison we build for ourselves from our identification with thoughts, emotions, beliefs, and desires. The demolition process begins as Premananda lovingly and humorously guides participants to see that they are not the experience 'my life', but rather the awareness in which the experience happens. He focuses his meetings on this awareness, the Self, which is our true nature and is revealed when the mind becomes quiet.

Five years before meeting Papaji, Premananda found a hand-tinted photograph in a room he was renting in his last years with Osho. Although he had no idea who this person was, the beautiful eyes gradually made their way into his heart and being. Later he discovered this was Ramana Maharshi, whose saintly presence and teaching of Self-enquiry, 'Who am I?' had made him famous.

On meeting Papaji he was deeply affected to see that he had the same photograph on his wall. Premananda sees himself as a messenger for the ancient wisdom of India, the wisdom that forms the basis of most spiritual traditions. He is deeply grateful to his direct masters and to many others in the East and West whom he has met and befriended through his project *Blueprints for Awakening*.

Premananda now lives between Cologne and Dusseldorf, Germany, in a residential Satsang and Arts Community of twenty people. The purpose of the community is to create a fertile ground for awakening. Satsang occurs in formal meetings and in the day-to-day life; it forms the core of the community. The most important part of the daily work is the work that happens inside each person. The work and working together create mirrors, giving constant reminders to look at what is happening inside.

The community is housed in a beautiful seventeenth century mansion, Open Sky House. There Premananda holds regular retreats and weekends. He has a closed Sangha group around him by his invitation, consisting of people who have a strong longing to become free. They meet with him on a regular basis. The community is open to anybody who has come to the point in their life where they want to know themselves – not their stories and dramas, but rather their true nature. 'Who am I?' is the focus of the community and the motto is 'be as you are'.

From his deep love for India, Premananda was led to meet and befriend many Indian saints and masters, collecting rare interviews which can now be found in his book and its companion film *Blueprints for Awakening – Indian Masters*. After the support and feedback he received, he was led to another book and film project *European Spiritual Masters – Blueprints for Awakening*. A third on USA and Australian masters is under preparation.

He has directed five films which can be seen with sub-titles in nine languages: Indian Masters and European Masters in the *Blueprints for Awakening* series and *Arunachala Shiva*, a film about the life and teachings of Sri Ramana Maharshi. Recently he completed *Satori*, a film on the awakening of a resident in his community. The film, *The Great Misunderstanding* is the companion to this book.

He enjoys art and beauty and is himself a painter. As an artist, Premananda has exhibited his paintings in India, Australia and Germany. They are in private collections in several countries. His joy-filled abstract paintings are an expression of the playfulness at the core of his being. They can be seen within this book. He encourages and facilitates many forms of creativity at Open Sky House.

He is actively available in this International Community to meet you as a guest or volunteer and to invite you to live with him if your passion for living in freedom is great enough. He offers on-line Satsang three evenings a week through Satsang TV, which can be viewed live around the world. You can engage in dialogue with him by entering into the meeting live. There is also a comprehensive archive of three hundred Satsang meetings since 2009, in seven different languages.

Premananda is no longer caught up in his conditioned mind, believing he is a somebody. Out of the emptiness, Self manifests as enormous energy and presence in each moment. Through his example, Premananda shows us that spiritual life is every moment. There is no 'spiritual life', there is just life. The whole effort is simply to be present for every moment.

He is an unusual character, full of fun and lightness with the possibility of a sudden storm at any moment. Many love him to bits and others find him outrageous. He is never boring but not always able to see when he is too much. He would love to invite you to come and make your own assessment!

www.premanandasatsang.org
www.premanandasatsangtv.org

ARUNACHALA PILGRIMAGE RETREAT

This Satsang Retreat is an opportunity to live in a community situation for three weeks at the holy mountain Arunachala in Tiruvannamalai, South India. Arunachala has been a powerful place of pilgrimage for two thousand years. We are accommodated in a lovely modern ashram. Our Satsang meetings take place on the roof directly overlooking the holy mountain. Each morning there is quiet meditation, yoga and Satsang. We spend the afternoons either alone, in Ramana Maharshi's ashram, or together with the group. Also, we go on a magical four day bus trip that brings us to four wonderful Indian Saints and allows us to see and experience Indian culture and landscape.

www.india.premanandasatsang.org

OPEN SKY PRESS
Timeless Wisdom

European Masters – Blueprints for Awakening is a bridge from the ancient texts and teachings of India and the East to today's modern Western life. Premananda interviews fourteen European spiritual Masters, some well-known others little-known. It's a joy to hear Nonduality explained in modern English and from a Western experience of life.

ISBN 978-0-9555730-7-1 Book
ISBN 978-0-9566070-1-0 DVD

Blueprints for Awakening – Indian Masters is an archive of rare and exceptional video, audio and print material, a marvellous collection of lively, authentic sage wisdom-teaching. British spiritual teacher Premananda uses the teachings of Sri Ramana Maharshi to compose twelve questions which he puts to sixteen Indian Masters.

ISBN 978-0-9555730-4-0 Book
ISBN 978-0-9555730-5-7 DVD

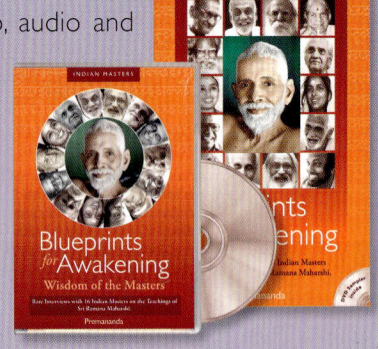

Arunachala Shiva is a profound homage to the spiritual greatness of Bhagavan Sri Ramana Maharshi who is one of India's most well-known Sages. Included in this book is his famous text, *Who Am I? (Nan Yar)* in which he declares that Self-enquiry is the most direct route to Self-realisation.

ISBN 978-0-9555730-6-4 Book
ISBN 978-0-9555730-9-5 DVD

Papaji – Amazing Grace is a book of fifteen profoundly beautiful interviews with people who had an Awakening with Papaji. They are stories of a housewife, a businessman, even an officer of a nuclear powered aircraft carrier. Each person, whatever their background, had the common longing to discover the eternal Truth of who they are. When this longing is strong enough a Master appears. 'Perfect Awakening is possible here and now for every human being, regardless of background, practice or personal circumstances. You are already free! Anything gained afresh will be lost. What is eternal is always within you, as your own Self.' Papaji

ISBN 978-0-9555730-0-2

Arunachala Talks consists of eight talks given spontaneously at Premananda's annual Arunachala Satsang Retreat in South India. Premananda lovingly and humorously guides us to see that we are not the experience 'my life', but rather the awareness in which the experience happens. The talks discuss the effects of devotion, trust and destiny, bringing us to presence.

ISBN 978-0-9555730-2-6

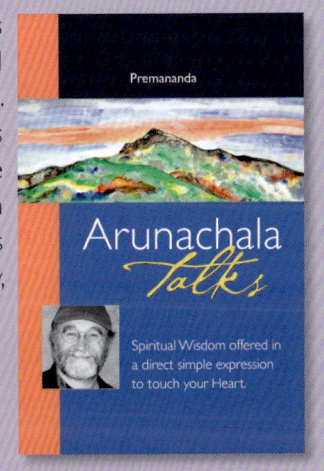

OPEN SKY PRESS
Publishers of Fine Quality Spiritual Books

Tel +49 (0) 2173 1016070   Fax +49 (0) 2173 4099205
office@openskypress.com
www.openskypress.com

New Companion Films

The Great Misunderstanding
Discover Your True Happiness With A Simple New Understanding

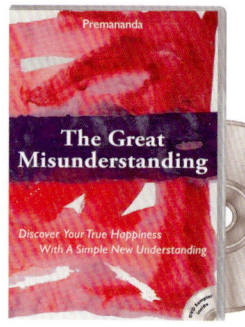

An intense experiment in conscious living: One spiritual teacher and twenty people with a strong longing for a true understanding of what is real, living together in one house. This film shows the residents in their search for Awakening, with Premananda guiding them from the misunderstanding of separation to oneness. He explains clearly how we are trapped in our conditioning and points us to our true nature.

ISBN 978-0-9570886-8-9

Satori
Metamorphosis of An Awakening

Rare footage of an awakening, traditionally called Satori. It can be a subtle shift or powerful and dramatic. Lakshmi, living around spiritual teacher Premananda, experienced this powerful energy phenomenon. In this film they dialogue about Lakshmi's experience of that moment and what has happened since.

ISBN 978-0-9570886-9-6

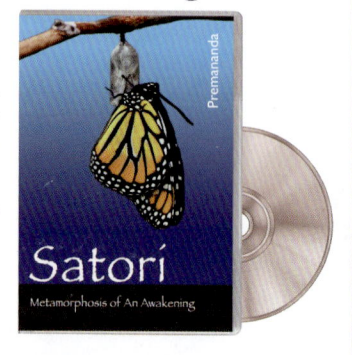

DVD Preview Sampler
Watch Trailers of New Companion Films
The Great Misunderstanding
Satori - Metamorphosis of An Awakening